REFLECTION *of* HUMAN BEHAVIOUR

D1832045

REFLECTION
of
HUMAN BEHAVIOUR

Impression, Emotion and Preception

Bholanath Das

Reflection *of* Human Behaviour

Rs. 690

© Bholanath Das

ISBN: 978-81-7835-763-8

All rights reserved. No Part of this book may be reproduced in any manner without written permission.

Published in 2009 in India by
Kalpaz Publications
C-30, Satyawati Nagar,
Delhi:-110052
E-mail: kalpaz@hotmail.com
Phone : 9212729499

Lasser Type Setting by: Quick Media, Delhi
Printed at : Young Art Press, Delhi - 92

for

parents, *Smt. Durga and Shri Fakir Charan Das* with obeisance

and

life-partner, *Sarswati* with love

Contents

If all difficulties were known at the outset of a long journey, most of us would not have started at all! - Anon

Preface

Imagination is more important than knowledge.

—Albert Einstein

The stories included in the book are crafted of lofty imagination blended with facts gleaned from real life and embellished. The fictionalization does not intend to offer an ephemeral insight arising out of preconceived or predetermined notion, but a reflection of the experiences, the social dynamics of power and grandeur to love and compassion sweeping over a vast tract of time and space. In the context that a literary work is primarily a product of enjoyment and pleasure for those who happen to read it, sincere attempt has been made to capture the reflections of sensitive human behaviour that encompasses feelings, responses, impressions, emotions as one voyages through life in the moments of highs and lows, hope and despair, anxieties and excitements, agony and ecstasy.

The stories include *'Bibhuti'* which a long story or a short novel. It is about an ordinary person; a natural leader, fiercely independent, often conveying piercingly sharp response to most things and ready to do or die for what he believed. His inexorable travail in this harsh world is a saga of intense struggle, a kaleidoscope of emotions in the mental, personal and psychosocial plane. His life and style, the principles he pursued are exceptional, sometimes beyond the common man's perspicacity. He lived the way he liked. The life reflects, in fact, very nearly the way it has turned out in print, factual in content and unbiased in presentation. I have taken few liberties in chronology and names are fictitious. The rest I could not have invented, had I tried.

The book also includes my children's contribution; *Bhim and Bhoi* (Kamalini), *Marriage in the Family* (Kavita), *Kitchen Blues* (Geeta), *Thank You, God!* (Kamal), duly edited.

As readers see behind the writer's mask, you would certainly identify yourselves with a moment, an event, a scene, a situation, a character, a circumstance of fact or fiction that coalesces. I will find you and your love when you would be ambling some where along the pages with me. And it would indeed be worth the effort and accomplishment. God willing, we shall meet on another journey, perhaps on a new path and to a new destination.

I welcome views from readers.
E-mail: dasbn@hotmail.com

1

Management in Treta

We promise accoding to our hopes.
We perform according to our fears. —*Francois*

Debashish (Deb) lived with his family in the metropolis Kolkata. He had a decent job with accommodation in the central part of the city. He hailed from a village in Orissa where his parents lived. He normally visited his parents on week ends and liked to travel by the super fast Dhauli Express from Howrah to Balasore. It was very convenient as it used to reach Balasore at 1000 Hrs and by noon he was at the dining table. In the process he developed a sort of relationship with the concerned persons in the air conditioned chair car in the train.

On one Saturday morning he reached Howrah station and, to his surprise, he heard the announcement that the train was cancelled. This was not very usual to the importance attached to this train. He was advised by some Railway staff that a fast passenger was scheduled to leave Howrah and it would reach Balasore before 1130 Hrs. He further added that the travel would be almost at one fourth the cost of the air conditioned chair car. Such advices at Kolkata were aplenty keeping in tune the socio-cultural ethos of the society.

Deb weighed the alternatives of returning skipping the weekend visit or to experience the hospitality of the Indian Railway's passenger train service at cheaper rate and delay by one and half hour. As the weather was very temperate he opted for the journey, bought a ticket and boarded the train.

The compartment of the train was reasonably clean, sparsely occupied with people leisurely spreading their limbs and belongings on the wooden planks. A part of the compartment occupied by a group of young people attracted his attention. He tried to make himself comfortable occupying a single seat adjoining the window, prepared to spend some time in the company of the young group next to him.

The buzz of the hawkers selling a variety of utilities and small gift items ranging from tea to pan masala and toys to pen sets gradually reduced and the train whistled to move. Deb looked forward to the five hours experience in this passenger train that would stop almost at all stations as against the super fast that had only one stop in the middle of his journey. He took out a magazine from the brief case and leafed through.

Among the group one person with a finely drawn ascetic face was saffron clad but surprisingly without any sandal wood paste or red *tilak* on the forehead. He was addressed Guruji by the other five who had normal attire of shirt and trouser. They were asking him to tell a nice story that would be of interest. He agreed and asked them to listen carefully and prepare for answering questions at the end. He prepared himself and began,

"Hope all of you know the story of Ramayana."

While all nodded in affirmation, he said, "All of us know Ravana as a bad person who kidnapped Sita, but do we know why?"

You may tell the story of Suparnakha and his action was to avenge the agony inflicted on her by Laxman; but the fact was different.

All gawked at him expectant to hear further. Deb has heard and read the story of Ramanaya himself. What could be the reason for Sita's kidnapping? He thought himself bewildered.

Guruji took a pause and intoned with eloquence, "I think you know that Lanka was an island with limited resources and the inhabitants were very poor. Ravana as their king was too eager for the upliftment of the lot. He was aware of the socio-economic affluence of the neighbouring country, 'Bharat'. He thought that development of Lanka would be possible only if their island could be linked with the main land and the people could have access to work there, learn the skills in various trades and earn a decent living."

His associates listened intently. However Guruji mentioned calmly to intervene if they had any questions or difficulties in understanding the story.

He then continued, "Ravana was looking for means to implement his strategy to link their island with Bharat. He knew that the only person capable of the completing the task was Rama. But the problem remained how to get his services. He learnt that Rama was roaming in the adjacent forest with his wife and brother. While he was in the process of evaluating various options, Supernakha's earnest request for protection from a brother against her injury sparked an evil ego that turned the noble plan to revenge. But

Ravana was shrewd enough not to loose sight of his plans. He decided to exploit the opportunity killing two birds with one stone. The evil idea came to his mind was to coerce Rama to build a bridge across that connected their island. This, he felt would satisfy his sister with a revenge and his objective accomplished."

Guruji declared a break for tea as they reached Kharagpur. In the mean time Deb was enured to the surroundings and totally absorbed in thought. A new Ramanaya was in the making! He was unaware of fact that they have travelled half distance through and reached Kharagpur. The passenger train must have stopped at many stations. A few minutes passed with noise of passengers alighting and boarding, vendors shouting to attract the attention of the buyers, relatives and friends seeing off their dear ones and those who continue their journey inside the train were busy sipping tea and watching their luggage. The train then whistled and slowly moved off the platform.

The bustle inside the compartment gradually reduced to chit chats in small groups. Guruji settled down after a visit to the change room. He mentioned with introspection that though every one of us read the epic hardly anyone cared to think why a person of the stature and nature of Ravana kidnapped Sita.

"It was Ravana's plan, as I explained earlier to get the island connected with the main land." he remarked.

One person among the group ventured to ask, "Did the end justify the means?"

Guruji thundered with his sonorous voice, "That is precisely my question. To what extent objective accomplishment could be the sole criteria with what ever means, as it is prevalent in the business and society at present."

He cited numerous examples of similar actions being taken by CEOs in business and politicians in present day society.

The discussion continued for some time and to Deb's surprise Guruji turned out to be well read and well versed with the modern management practices, besides his deep insight to the mythology. Deb was hesitating to intervene and seek certain clarification, as he did not know any of them. And when he finally decided to ask, the train stopped at a small station and the group along with the saffron clad Guruji got down.

The interesting interpretation offering a new dimension to the personality of Ravana kept Deb occupied for quite some time as if he was enthralled. The train came to a grinding halt and people started getting down and getting in with commotion, the familiarity of the station reminded him of Balasore. He looked out through the window and noticed that he has indeed reached his destination. He quickly picked up his brief case, alighted and went for the next mode of conveyance to reach home. While he was passing through the usual lanes he thought of the journey and was happy to conclude that what he expected to be a prosaic experience turned to exhilarating.

Deb's arrival and the sound of opening of the main gate relieved his parents of the anxieties. As he was explaining the reason for the delay, the lunch was served and he joined. His father, Barada Prasanna was known for his erudition in *kathas, puranas and Upanishads*. Deb narrated his experience and the new dimension of Ravana as explained by the saffron clad Guruji. His father calmly remarked that means were equally important as the ends, notwithstanding the noble objective of Ravana. He was truly confused with ends and means. It was not justifiable at any cost. The lesson would continue to influence the human behaviour in time to come.

Some of his friends dropped in for usual chit-chat over a cup of tea late afternoon and Deb was too eager to narrate his experience in the passenger train. One of his friend claimed to be researching in ancient history mentioned that political manoeuvres by emperors for tactical gains were not uncommon. For example, Constantine's official endorsement of Jesus as the Son of God was to take advantage of His substantial influence on humanity and further unification of the Roman Empire. Jesus became the deity of divinity for the entire world. This not only precluded further pagan challenge to Christianity but the followers of Christ were able to redeem themselves only via the sacred channel - the Roman Catholic Church.

Another friend interjected, "The Guruji you are referring to must be a practising management guru on his way to conduct workshop in some corporate house."

And all burst into laughter.

2

A Goat Committed Suicide

In the naked light I saw ten thousand people,
May be more, People taking without speaking, People hearing without listening,
People writing songs that voices never heard,
No one dares disturb the sound of silence.

– Simon, G.

It was a bit late than normal routine for Ashutosh to reach home after a day's work. His anxious wife has already seen the wall clock a number of times, rechecked with his son's time piece on the study table and was waiting with the door opened and ajar. Ashutosh entered the living room, kept his brief case on the credenza and sat down on the sofa to relax when his son came jumping on him and started channel surfing in spite of mother's warning to keep quiet. The news reader of the 'SS News' mentioned that she would bring a unique story - how the 'Instant Adalat' at Anandgarh adjudged that a goat committed suicide, after the break.

The name Anandgarh touched a sensitive chord and spurred Ashutosh's mind. This is the village where he has spent his childhood. The unprecedented news of suicide by an animal that too an innocent goat attracted his attention. He asked his son, “Let’s see what it is all about.” While the channel continued with advertisement, his wife joined with two cups of coffee and biscuits.

The news correspondent began the story with a glimpse of the scenic beauty of the coastal village showing large water mass with ripples reflecting the golden rays of the afternoon spring sun. Palm trees popping up amidst peepul, mangoes and a host of local species scattered in a tropical pleasance enhanced the scenery. The camera finally focussed on the dead goat lying on side of a road passing through one corner of the pond. His nostalgic memory was eidetic where every house reminded a story and every lane a memory.

The story unfolded with the introduction of Niranjan, the owner of the ill fated goat. Niranjan is a young boy of about eighteen years. He lived with his grand mother (Maa) in a small cottage and the goat was their only possession. As he lost his parents in early age, Maa brought him up by seer hard work. And ‘Tripathy sir’ one of his teachers in the village High School has been his mentor.

It was around 3.30 in the afternoon. The village was returning back to normal activity after siesta; workers going for the second shift, women folk readying for usual chores – preparing evening snacks and dinner when Niranjan took his goat for some fresh fodder of green leaves from the branches of the trees on the side of the pond. No sooner did he get a few branches of tender leaves and started feeding the goat with affection, he heard a call from ‘Tripathy sir’, “Niranjan, do me a favour. I urgently need some medicine. It would be available in 'Sudha Chemist'. Take this bike, prescription and money. I am waiting for you here."

The medicine store being on the other side of the village, Niranjan fondly patted his pet, asked him not to move away and hurried. He reached the store, parked his bicycle along with a few others and went inside the store. As there were other customers, he waited for his turn. It must be about fifteen minutes he left the store with medicines. He picked up his bike and started walking. By the time he reached the main road and was about to ride, he realised that his purse was not in his pocket. He then put the bike to stand in a hurry near by a person busy with cycle repairing and almost ran to the store.

He brushed his shoulder with a lady and wanted to express his regret, "Ma (mother)...", the lady sternly quipped, "Bastard" settled her dress and proceeded ahead. While Niranjan was in a fix for a moment, an elderly person standing near by intoned, "You have addressed her as mother and she preferred to call you a bastard is a reflection on her character. Don't worry, my boy. This is life."

As he reached the shop, the chemist saw him and returned his purse with a smile and remark, "Do remember, haste is waste." He swallowed his remark and quickly retraced back. But to his surprise he noticed that the cycle was not in the place he kept. He looked around and ventured to ask the cycle repairer if he noticed any body taking his bike.

"Oh yes, a similar looking person took the bike." he replied.

"How can another person be similar to me?" was his question.

As there was no response from the man and his assistant, he asked again,

"Could you please tell me in which direction he went?"

"We have business to do. We can't waste time to look for directions."

Niranjan was so agonised that he felt like snubbing him but decided otherwise. The other person asked with sardonic smile, "Are you going to chase him if I tell you the direction?" Aghast, he wanted to punch and flatten his nose or hammer his head on the nearest wall, but could do nothing as he had other priorities. He stood there bewildered for a moment. While he was thinking what Tripathy sir would think of him, he saw a young man came along riding his bike, alighted and inquired if he was looking for the cycle. To the suggestion that he should have at least informed taking the bike, he nonchalantly remarked that he felt the urge to go round and utilised the bike which was readily available.

'All is well that ends well' he thought and decided to keep the issue at rest. He rushed back to gain the time lost in these uncalled for encounters. He saw from a distance an unusual crowd on the side of the pond and eyed for Tripathy sir as he reached the place. Everybody was busy talking, shouting and perhaps nobody cared to listen. In a moment Tripathy sir came, touched his shoulder and as it appeared failed to find words to comfort him for his irreparable loss. He knew how Niranjan cossetted the goat as his treasured possession. A young urchin came and shouted, "Niranjan Bhai, your goat has been crushed by the lorry. Do come and see for yourself."

He hesitatingly proceeded, accompanied by a few sympathisers and Tripathy sir. He instantly felt very sad at the pathetic site of his loving companion and experienced a pang of regret for leaving it.

No sooner did he regain his composure, Jaganna (a sobriquet derived from his name, 'Jagatananda' and 'nana' a respect for an elder) arrived in the scene and took the centre stage. Jaganna needed no introduction to the village folk. He was a Brahmin performing death ceremonies and occasionally conducted tours of elderly persons to Kashi, Godavari, Kolkata, Baidyanath Dham, Puri and the like. With his experience of travelling few places outside the state he had picked up Hindi a little and had developed relationship with transporters which no other person in the village had. He sat down on a stone accompanied by some of his coteries and declared, "Well, this is an unprecedented case in our village history that a goat has been killed by a rushing lorry and that the goat means a lot for the poor family." The shouting, talking gradually reduced to a murmur and finally ceased. Jaganna enthroned himself as the arbiter of the impromptu Adalat and made a bold statement, "We will soon punish the guilty. But the circumstances that led to this require in-depth analysis. All concerned would be given opportunity to share what they know about the accident/incident. The decision will be taken logically, impartially and true to the fact." One from the group seated alongside called, "Niranjan, please come here."

Niranjan wrapped up in his own trepidation and speculation could hardly pay attention to the call. His teacher was standing by and cautioned him, "The snake-in- the grass is on the prowl. Be careful as you talk to them"

"So, yours is a special goat?" asked Jaganna.

"Yes, very special to me and Maa, as you know sir."

"Why you feel it is so special to you?"

Silence prevailed.

"Is it your pet?"

"Yes, sir."

"How do you call it?"

"Sir, ..."

"So, you do not have a fond name for your pet. But usually people do call their pets with nick names.".

"I call my cat, Rani." A girl from the gathering said.

"My dog is Raja" another person mentioned.

"Our cow is Kamadhenu, our bulls are ...." continued.

Jaganna surveyed the mood of the people present and clearing his throat asked again, "What special food you have given today to your special pet?"

Again silence...

"I usually have mutton for my Raja." The dog owner said.

"I cooked fish for my pet, Rani" shouted the girl boastfully.

"Special fodder and oil cakes for the cow are routine now" continued another.

Niranjan sighed, feeling helpless, impotent to translate his concern into answer he desperately needed. While a volley of questions continued he was buried in thought. He felt as though a thousand devils were conspiring against him. He lamented, "What in God's name have I done to deserve this?"

He wanted suddenly to lash out something or somebody not only to inflict pain in retaliation against the savage manner that was meted to him but to hurt himself, for he felt himself responsible for all this.

After a brief consultation with his associates, Jaganna delivered the ad-judgement, "Ladies and gentlemen, may I with the permission of all conclude:

The facts suggest that the goat has been leading a pathetic life; no fond name, no good food, no personal care and that led it to be under depression. Consequently the forces of the circumstances drove it to end its life to be relieved of the continued agony. And therefore it would be logical for the 'Instant Adalat' to decree that the goat committed suicide."

The monstrosity of the decision slashed him like physical blow amidst the stunning silence that prevailed. His throat burned with heartening impulse to cry welled within him. His grand mother came rushing to the middle of the crowd and cried with charged emotion. Her cry remained unheard of amidst the noise that arose as people started dispersing. Some heard her say, "How much money have you taken from the truckwallah? God will certainly punish you for the sinful act."

The reporter focussing on Niranjan standing in supplication concluded, "While Niranjan remained reticent one could only notice the touch of tears that slowly would have coursed across his cheek."

Ashutosh too felt emotionally hurt and almost in monotone, "So indifferent. So unconcerned. Not even one objection. I would not even imagine it is possible in my village." And to his surprise his wife remarked, "Time has changed, dear!" And he looked on...

3

Un-Common Man

If you can find humour in anything,
even poverty, you can survive it.

—Bill Cosby

The morning was indeed beautiful in Padmapur after an unusual spell of drizzle and chill. The sun shone in its full strength with flood of radiance and delight for all. The untainted sky hung like a vault of pure sapphire over the land mass beneath. One and all woke up to life and activity. The birds soared, the cattle moved to fields for fabulous grazing, the young ones gathered for a game, women busied in spreading wet clothes to dry and elderly needed a cosy seat to bask in the sun.

And this small village was in possession of the individual to whom Nityananda Bholan (writer 'Nitai') was journeying. He felt the fatigue of the over night journey by the state transport corporation on rural road disappeared. He was about to reach the large farm house, surrounded by a variety of plants, stock of paddy and a cow shed. The thought of completing his dream project and offer the world a literary master piece was exhilarating. It was a moment of ecstasy after a long toil.

The whole process of selection of the subject to the final draft in his hand over a period of almost four years mirrored like paintings on a broad canvas. The Basant Panchami day of 2001. Unsuccessful to find an avenue for breakthrough that would catapult him to fame after fifteen years of writing Nitai almost reached a point of depression when wife Bhanu Priya broached in to convey that he should write a novel on the life of a common man that had some peculiar un- commonness. "Literature is full of biographies of great man. Create some thing unique. A treatise on a common man who has excelled in life." she explained.

Nitai was too excited at the great idea as a gift from the Goddess *Saraswati* and set out to detailed planning. The selection of a so called common man was no easy task. It entailed development of a suitable model for eliciting response and scientific approach to selection. He decided to leave no stone unturned and take help from his friends knowledgeable in their respective disciplines. After all he has to come up with a master piece. He has many friends now who enjoy high reputation as Readers in colleges. Nitai remembered when his friends took teaching as a profession and he declined such offers on completion of Ph. D. His yearning for creative work in literature drove him to pursue a career in writing.

He discussed the issue with friends, evaluated the inputs and drafted a suitable letter for mailing. He also collected electoral rolls, selected a random list with expert advice and mailed for response. He addressed the village *sarpanchs* for nominating one or two persons with extraordinary qualities and capabilities.

He was overwhelmed with the huge response. The task of selection imposed on him awesome responsibility and by mid 2002 he could arrive at the final decision that the hero of his novel would be Shri Surya Pratap Das Chaudhury (Choudhurysaab) of Padmapur. Though there were a few more equally promising candidates, Chaudhurysaab was clearly outstanding with his uncommon experiences and achievements. A few such are shared with the readers.

One of his uncommon experience: one and all would cherish the nostalgic memories of the childhood days. The reminiscences of Chaudhurysaab's experience and impression were to the contrary. He firmly believed this period is sans freedom and he loved freedom the most. While children normally would feel drugged with happiness of embrace and tighten their arms for eternity, he narrated a few encounter with certain devilish aunties chewing *paan* with tobacco and red spit oozing out from the corner of the lips show their love by embracing and kissing that drove him nouseating. In some other occasion when he would love to sleep, his grand mother insisting for the fractured rhyme she sometimes enjoyed without understanding how he was deprived of personal enjoyment.

And his uncommon achievement. He was too unhappy with the result of his twin sons when they were not allowed to appear in the Board examination for passing High School for the second time. While his boys were given the required attention their inherent weakness in a foreign language like English which no one around speaks stood in their way. Apropos detailed deliberation he advised the boys to pray the head master for sympathy and at least allow them to appear leaving the result to Almighty. The head master was so strict that he felt it would be partial to allow them leaving others. And to appease the boys and divert their attention he asked them to find at least one coin with head on both the side for considering their request. The boys unaware of the implication of the message requested their father for help. Chaudhurysaab took it as a challenge and got two coins made with the help of a mechanical workshop in town. The boys presented the coins as part of their bargain and finally the head master had to keep his promise. Although success remained a distant dream, the twins had the satisfaction of appearing the Board examination.

During the past two years Nitai has taken the trouble to visit Chaudhurysaab a number of times and today he has come prepared for finalisation of the project he has been engaged with for almost five years. He has obtained consent of his wife Bhanu Priya for a bit longer absence, if required. He has also come with the report on the status of the ventures taken up by his two sons with reasons of failure and suitable revival plan for both of them.

During the last visit he had to accept the assignment as a part of bargain and returned without much of his work as Choudhurysaab was too upset with his sons' performance. While he did mention during the course of interaction that his sons, Karan and Arjun were a bit weak in English, Niati was flummoxed with their wisdom and understanding. He only wished they were present to discuss and Choudhury Saheb would appreciate and accept simple suggestions.

Well, to cut the long story short, Karan and Arjun both failing to pursue higher studies as they could not pass high school in spite of the fact that – left no stone unturned, Karan went for training in automobiles and Arjun choose to learn tricks of conducting a business with one of their relatives. Finally Karan set up a garage and Arjun a Resturant in the town for the last three years. And as luck would have it, they are still living on the monthly maintenance budget received from father regularly. To begin with Nitai too was surprised as he knew of a number of flourishing enterprises in the town with such business. His investigation, however surprisingly revealed that the boys are not only pernickety but aho flibbertigibbet to perceive and appreciate very simple things.

The name board of Karan's garage mentions "Old Vehicles are not accepted" in bright red and the vehicle owners are reluctant to enter for repair. Similarly Arjun's restaurant indicates brightly "Guests not welcome" and as a result no one enters. And they have solid arguments and well thought of reasons for such display. Karan strongly feels that he has set up a sophisticated and modern garage not to waste his time on the repair of old junks but only the new model vehicles. And Arjun is of the view that every day a number of their relatives are in the town and he would not afford to entertain such guests. Both of them have deliberated and consciously decided for such display.

Nitai was about to reach his destination. The usual ambiance however was lacking. The road was deserted with a strange and subduing melancholy seemed to hang over it. It might be a deception to his fancy, but he thought the looks of the persons more and more shadowed with melancholy than he had ever witnessed on any previous occasion. He reached the farm house and threaded through the plaintive congregation.

"What happened?" he inquired.

"A bolt from the blue, sir. Choudhurysaab is no more." was the reply.

"Oh God! And how did he die?" cried Nitai deeply agitated

"That no one knows yet." answered an old man who stood by.

Tears rolled on his cheek as he entered the mansion of sorrow. The atmosphere in the residence was gripped by dolour. He saw the relict and the weeping family and failed to find words to comfort them.

The sudden demise of Choudhurysaab leaving behind his wife Kuntala Devi (Kunti), mother and two sons Karn and Arjan created a void that couldnot be filled. It was a catastrophe for the family. The family members have never bothered about any affairs - the obedient wife looking after domestic chores, sons only arrived yesterday from the town and the octogenarian mother deified. Choudhurysaab commanded unquestioned authority over all affairs in the village including his family. The members of the family and their near ones were intuitive how to face the future in the absence of the sole man of the family. They knew their shortcomings, but they have to shoulder the burden and endeavour to eke out a living out of a surreal. Necessity being the mother of invention, the present problem stirred them.

The last rites have to follow as per the customs. The arrangements were made and with usual chanting of hymn the last journey was conducted to the burning place. Unusual though, every one present became emotional and philosophical. Some of them were busy with funereal pyre others sitting and standing. Prolonged silence followed with sadness that pervaded the whole scene for some time. In the mean while gossip generated.

One felt, "Choudhury Saheb was a perfect gentleman. He acted with the dictum, 'heart within and God's over head."

"Well, can heart be outside and God underground?" was a tarse response from behind.

"Do you know how did he exalt himself from 'Das'to'Das Choudhury' ?"quipped another.

"He was too miser, I know." said some one.

"But no one ever goes empty handed from their house." came from his neighbour.

"That goes to the credit of Ma (Kunti). She is Annapurna." replied their servant.

As the flame grew to ashen the physical body there appeared a schism with intense debate that brought fore other shades on his personality Niati was not aware of. He felt apoplectic as his work remained incomplete. He forced himself to look composed, went to the boys, embraced them and prayed for His blessings at this hour of calamity. He only wished wisdom would prevail on them for taking right decision and tread the right path.

The group was to return to the farm house and Nitin slow and heavy with unquenched sleep, unlimited desperations decided to return to the bus stop. Absorbed in thoughts galore he took a seat on the wooden plank of the tea stall and ordered a cup of tea with a few pieces of short bread biscuits. The writer within him swirled to search the truth to pen the 'other side of personality of the un-common man'.

He felt wild excitement with whispering sweetness as he resolved with determination to present the world a literary master piece, come what may! And reflected, 'life is but a journey to the unknown.'

4

Grandpa Weds

The greatest battles of life are fought daily in the silent chambers of the soul.

David O McKay

Life has become too difficult for Bijoy too soon. The unexpected news from the market that his grandpa is all set for a new wedding puzzled him. He fidgeted in his room for so long but felt as if time has stopped for him. The usual affluence of life, a certainty of flow has ceased, home comfort has gone, its warmth has gone, the pleasant home appeared to him like a collection of cold bricks. He felt the need for meeting Kamal and share his problem. Though he was a few years elder they had grown up together as friends sharing their pleasure and pain. They felt at home together and confided with each other their personal secrets.

Bijoy had the impression that he would be available at home by 4 pm after the college and he searched for him three times during the last one hour. And this time, as no one responded to his call, he ventured to enter the house and over heard exchanges between his mother and wife. He safely concluded that Kamal must have gone to the place he normally visited when he felt disturbed. It was a few furlongs away from the habitat on the side of a rivulet. There existed a temple structure amidst the tropical pleasance. The place, despite human indifference and persecution provided an aura of sacredness and was his choice for solace in desperate moments.

As he walked along, he remembered how happily he had spent his life in the family but for yesterday and today. Even when his father died in an accident he received so much love, affection and attention from his grandpa that he forgot the sad moments. He cherished and his friends envied their happy family under the able leadership of his grandpa, Rudra Pratap Choudhury. His mother's devotion for smooth running of the household affairs, brother's sober demeanour, bhabiji's affection and above all wife's love combined to provide a heavenly experience at home. Though the problem of getting a job occasionally worried him but he enjoyed life to the full.

As expected, he found him sitting on a stone, with eyes closed in a meditative posture.

"Ah, there you are..." he announced and continued.

"Do you know that the whole town is abuzz with a story that my grandpa weds?"

Kamal could not perceive the situation, but knowing his nature, replied,

"Well, I have been a bit preoccupied with extra classes that I could not visit your place for the past few days. But what is the provocation for a sudden decision to get married at this age?"

"That is the precise point and I require your help."

He knew that Bijoy knew no moderation in his requests and impulses, and he yielded,

"I am ready to help in what ever manner you want, but..."

"The whole family is in a fix how to face the situation. We are disturbed. When I went to market in the morning, the tailor said that grandpa has ordered dresses for him and the lady, he has also placed orders for sweets, and food etc. and the pandit has also been asked to report day after tomorrow." Bijoy segued.

"Please tell me the whole story, when and how you came to know all this."

"I am sorry. Let me begin from the beginning."

"Well, every thing was normal till day before yesterday, that is Saturday, but grandpa did not return home that night. We all waited for dinner till late at night, made enquiries from his friend's house but there was no idea where he was. He did not inform anybody that he was going out of town. On Sunday morning brother and myself visited various places including the hospital to gather information about him. He however suddenly appeared by about 4 pm along with a lady. He desired that she would stay with us for a few days. And arrangements were made for her stay along with my mother. As you know, there is no extra room available now for guests, and mother is very touchy about who she is. Grandpa has not yet made anything clear who she is, why she is here etc. I am puzzled to learn from different people in market that he is planning to get married. Since then we are all upset. Mother feels shy to talk to that lady in this regard and bhabiji, my wife too cannot dare interfere. I wanted to talk to you and take your advice."

Listening to the imminent and complex problem Kamal forgot his own. He was baffled to the extent that threatened his perspicacity. He knew Choudhuty Saheb as a very rational person. He wondered if, of late he has developed some fancies. It could lead to complexities. His psychology lessons reminded him 'nothing is more insidious than the evolution of wishes from mere fancies and of wants from mere wishes.' He evaluated various possibilities and ruled out this aspect since he perceived him as an open minded man and maintained high moral values with high standard of ethics. Then how come sudden appearance of a lady in his life at this age and decision for immediate marriage!

"There is nothing to worry about. Let's face the situation square one." He tried to encourage Bijoy.

"What do we do now?"

"Let me think about it in cool mind. You discuss with your brother and mother. We need to ascertain the reason for such drastic action. I will try to reach your place before dinner time and shall talk to grandpa."

They returned in silence, each buried in thoughts. When Kamal reached home it was getting dark. His mother asked, "Where had you been since return from college? Bijoy was anxiously looking for you. Any thing serious..? Well, you get fresh, and we'll have tea."

He briefly washed and sat down calmly. His wife came with the tea tray. All three of them took a cup each. Breaking the silence his mother again queried, "You have not changed. Are you going out again?" she paused and continued. "How are Bijoy and his family? It is long since we met."

"Well, their problem is too complex. Bijoy says his grandpa came home day before yesterday with a lady and 'grandpa weds' information is in the air. And they are too scared to discuss with him."

He added, "While I don't believe this, I promised Bijoy to ascertain from grandpa. Please go ahead with dinner. I may be late."

They all felt concerned for the unusual happening.

Kamal reached, extended his regards and as expected he noticed great anxieties on every one's face. An eerie situation, lull before a storm!

"I shall discuss with grandpa. He is a very nice person and we'll find some solution." said he.

It was after 10.30 pm grandpa returned. Kamal paid obeisance and surprisingly found him quite normal as he used to be. All including the lady had dinner together. The ladies folk gradually repaired to their respective rooms.

"It is quite late, now. Please drop Kamal by the scooter." Grandpa asked Bijoy.

"Grandpa, I want to talk to you. It is very important." he politely submitted.

"I know, I know..since you are here at this time, I guess you must have something very urgent."

"If you permit, we sit down comfortably on the sofa and discuss." he suggested.

They sat down. Moments passed by. While he was thinking how to approach the sensitive subject without hurting the feelings of the person he respected, grandpa calmly narrated the reason for his decision for the new arrangement he has thought of. He explained that the grandsons, their wives are busy in their affairs and he is left all alone. And that he has found a lady of compatible age to be his life partner, all should welcome this. He also assured that his love for all would continue to be same and rather they would receive the love and affection of a grand mother, in addition.

"I hope you would also endorse the decision, Kamal." he concluded.

Grandpa's clear and cogent statement of his thinking caught them unaware. He suddenly felt ill at ease. He wanted to gain some time to know the views of Bijoy, his brother and his mother.

"We respect your decision. You have been the guiding light for all of us and we are sure you will certainly take the right step." affirmed Kamal.

He found both the brothers apoplectic and in a bid to divert from the bizarre scenario requested grandpa that Ajoy and Bijoy should discuss with mother, too.

"Well, by all means." quipped grandpa.

Dazed brothers parted without a word leaving him with grandpa. Neither spoke for some time. Even at this late hour, Kamal did not feel sleepy. His mind was too preoccupied. He mustered courage and asked, "Grandpa, are you really serious?"

"I should not subject you to more stress on this non issue. I realise your concern as a true friend."

The statement was more of confusion than solution for him. He kept on brooding over and waited for the brothers. It seemed almost eternity and there was no sign of their return. Grandpa yawned and felt fatigued. He then called him said softly, "Don't take this seriously. It is just a drama. I wanted to test how my children feel for me and the lady who is a stage artist plotted this."

He felt speechless. He just could not believe that all the seriousness was simply a melodrama. He wanted to call Ajoy and Bijoy and inform, but grandpa would not allow. They waited ... After almost one and half hour they came totally wreck.

"Any problem?" asked grandpa.

"As you are our guide and philosopher, we accept your decision. We will respect her as our grand mother, as you wish. We are at your command, ready to carry out your orders." the brothers almost chorused.

Grandpa could not stand any more. He, emotionally charged, eyes filled with tears spoke in a hushed tone that he was sure of the values the children have and they stood the test. He hugged them affectionately and kissed their fore head.

"How could you think that your grandpa would do such thing at this age? Should you have not talked to me?"

"They were too shy to interact with you and therefore Bijoy discussed with me. Hope you would pardon me for intrusion and them for their child like behaviour." Kamal said in trepidation.

"Oh, no you are also my child. It is all ok. I am so happy. I feel accomplished that my mission is complete. But, I realise that I should not have gone that far." He intoned.

The sombre feelings vanished and the brothers flushed with a spark of spirit. Kamal pushed them to go inside and inform the ladies.

"Your night has been spoilt for us and unnecessary thing like this." grandpa told.

"Grandpa, you have always been our ideal - the pristine purity of dharma." he mentioned.

Grandpa called Bijoy and asked him to leave Kamal at home. Though he felt like asking the need for such a drama, he decided otherwise. When they were walking in the silent hours, Kamal was reminded of the important saying 'All is well that ends well.' As they reached almost midway to his home he asked Bijoy to return wishing better days ahead with the promises of morning sun.

5

Saraswathi *alias* Sarah

There is no agony like an untold story inside of you.

—Maya Angelou

This was Frankfurt in mid 1980s, the residence of Narendra Kamal. He lived with his wife, Vidya, eleven year old daughter and son who recently celebrated his fifth birthday. He was on Foreign Service with assignment as Investment Adviser for the promotion and facilitation of non resident Indian investment from Europe. In course of his efforts to publicize the policies and special facilities Government offered to encourage investment, he has been meeting the Indians through Indian associations in various locations in Europe. And he used to host official parties on occasions for enhancing the presence of the office and gain some advantage in networking with people who mattered.

One such dinner was organized on the Friday before Christmas. The first snowing of the season started with unexpected heavy snow. The guests confirmed earlier attended, but requested to leave early due to such inclement weather. By 8.30 pm all European guests left after coffee or cognac. For the Indian families, it was an opportunity to meet, talk on purchases, parties slated, plans regarding their visit to homeland and such like. The ladies group got emotionally engaged and to separate them for lonely homes was rather difficult for the men folk. As the weather worsened, they too reluctantly parted company.

It has been tiring for their daughter to leave all these guests from gate to parking, family by family, accompanying with umbrella. She came and informed, "Maa, everybody has left. It's snowing heavy. Pray, they don't have problem on way."

"Thanks a lot. Join with aunty and have something you like. I don't think you have you eaten well with others." Her mother said matter-of- factly.

"No thanks. Let me wash and sleep."

"Please arrange the bed for aunty in the guest room and then you are free."

As the lone guest, Saraswathi was sitting and waiting, she requested, "Aunty, I'll show you our temporary home and the guest room."

She took her along, showed her bed and other rooms.

"Please call me if you need anything. I am next to your room." She said and left.

Vidya was at the table clearing some space for them to dine comfortably. She said, "You have been more a host than guest. I am grateful for the troubles you have taken. You too must be tired. Let's have something."

They talked intimately while eating. She found her quite amiable to gel with others so soon. During interaction, she however realized that she was not happy and wanted to tell something, may be personal and hesitating. The dinner ended with some sweets as usual.

While leaving the table, Vidya enquired, "I think, you would like to have coffee. I'll get for you."

And she followed to say, "No, thanks. Madam. I had enough."

"I thought, staying here so long, you must have developed European habits."

"It is after ages that I have the opportunity to eat something I savor. My stomach is full."

"I'll pack something for your husband tomorrow. Please do remind me."

Kamal in the mean time entered the bed room for changing to night dress and searched his pajama. He did not like to disturb his wife for such trivial matter as, he felt, she must be too tired with the arrangements without any assistance. He felt happy the way the children behaved. They are growing to be assets. And suddenly he remembered his discussion that ended with Saraswati's invitation.

"Sir, please excuse me for disturbing you." His secretary Yuvanhoe rang.

"Anything urgent?"

"No sir. Here is one Frau Sarah Schneider who insists to talk to you."

"I don't think I know her."

"But she says she knows you and wants to talk to you personally."

"Well, in that case, let me talk to her."

"Sir, good afternoon. I am Saraswathi from Lower Saxony. I met you at Hanover Fair along with my husband. And I came all the way to specifically meet you and seek your advice. I need your help."

"You could have taken an appointment. I am too busy now and it is rather not possible to meet and discuss."

"I am sorry. But I desperately solicit your guidance and assistance."

"I don't understand. Anything official could only be done after the holidays. You know Europe closes for almost a week during this period." Kamal explained.

"I could, with great difficulty, get permission for today's visit. I'll come immediately. Please do spare me a few minutes." She pleaded with supplication.

He thought over and asked, "Are you alone? When do you plan to return?"

"I have permission to stay here tonight. Shall return tomorrow morning."

"In that case, please join us in the get together being arranged here tonight. In case you like, you may stay with us and leave as per your plan. We'll have sufficient time after dinner to talk to."

As she instantly agreed, he instructed the secretary to extend an invitation along with direction to reach without problem.

He also recalled that he only told his wife about her stay, but not regarding her request to discuss something of which he,too had no idea. He went to the kitchen where both the ladies were busy talking.

"Vidya, the purpose of Saraswathi's coming here tonight, which I have not informed you, is to discuss some urgent matter. Please do us a favour. Organize a cup of tea for me and what ever she wants before you retire. You must be tired, but we'll not get better time as she would leave in the morning." He requested.

"If you have no objection, I'll join you. Please be comfortable in the living room. I am getting tea and coffee."

"Tea is okay for me, too. And I am sorry for imposing as a guest and intruding your private space." Saraswathi was apologetic.

Kamal followed by Saraswathi left the room and settled on the sofa. In a few minutes, his wife joined them with a tray of tea and some potato wafers.

"Your kids are too cute and obedient." Saraswathi began.

"We are proud of them. Even at this tender age they have started appreciating the necessity to help. And all credit goes to the mother."

"You have also helped her a lot, in the absence of my secretary. Our sincere thanks." He continued.

"And please do tell me frankly your problem. In case I would be of any help, I'll certainly do what ever is possible."

"I'll not take much of your time; but I must briefly tell from the beginning. It relates to my life. I am at a cross road. I have been longing to say so much and my eyes have been searching through the window of the mind someone who would at least listen. I think I will be able to get some solace."

While she said eyes riveted to the ground, Mr. and Mrs. Kamal exchanged glances bewildered. And Mrs Kamal intervened saying, "Tea is ready. Please take and feel free to tell what ever is worrying you. I am sure, you will shed some of your burden."

Wrapped in gloom, eyes brimming she began,

"I was born in a desolate environment of a suburb of Madras, a world of silent allure; where dreams fade as quickly as dusk to a dark night, aspirations remain as obscure reflection in memories and thoughts leave their imprints on the fabric of life with no scope for colours; when bleak present disables the days to move into the future. Against such a background, my father died soon after my birth. My mother worked hard for sustenance and financing my education. Father D' Souza of the neighbourhood church helped us a lot. I completed my graduation. While friends of my age got married and settled in life, I continued to be a burden to my mother all due to my complexion. Boys preferred fair skin, as a matter of pride. I cursed myself not as much for my lack of beauty, as to the cause of mother's anxieties.

A day came in my life. It was Easter celebration in the church when I actively helped father in the event. As usual many boys too joined and one of them was a European who also came along with others. He was studying at Madras under some exchange programme. After the programme was over, he in the presence of Father D' Souza asked my mother if she would be willing to consider my marriage with him. Mother was in a fix and I could not gather my wits to respond instantly to such a proposal which I could never imagine to happen.

"Please do consider seriously, Durga." Advised excited Father D' Souza.

I thought of asking his background, the reason for taking such a decision as we do not know each other; but Father intervened, "It's Lord's wish. He has listened to your prayer and sent this boy. Saraswathi will be very happy to live in Germany."

He convinced my mother that it was the best possible opportunity for me and she too agreed, suppressing her emotion to part the only company she had. Our marriage was solemnized in the church according to the catholic rites. We were declared man and wife. And by about three months, the passport and visa formalities were completed. His programme in India also came to an end and we reached his house in Lower Saxony.

A new chapter of my life began. I have nurtured some dreams, though amidst uncertainty arising out of lack of information on a different land, new culture and a difficult language I would have to learn. In any case, I was determined to strive for adjustment and adaptation. I had no alternative. But sadly my euphoria dampened. I realized that I was lost in the mist of time and space.

To begin with I requested for learning the language so that I could communicate properly. My husband and my in-laws felt it was not necessary. The expressed opinion was that I should pick up gradually. And I had to agree.

I also realized that the family was in a penurious state in the local standard. The family depended on limited income by his father and my husband was in search of a job. It was difficult for them and I joined. They perhaps considered me as additional burden to the family. As I came from difficult economic background, it was nothing new and I tried to convince them that I was willing and ready to share pleasure and pain as a member of the family. But their indifferent behaviour continued. I felt, I was totally isolated.

I was not allowed to cook, under the pretext that I did not know their recipe. And at the same breath, no one cared even to ask me whether I liked the food or not. For the change of my citizenship, my name has been changed to Sarah. And if I narrate my plight, it would take days. I may sum up saying that I lost everything: my nationality, my name, my society, my near and dear ones, my culture and above all my identity.

Sometimes violent storm rages in me that could madden even the beasts with its eerie chaos, but yet I have not informed my mother, which I cannot afford. I feel, at her age she needs support and not anxieties."

They have been listening with rapt attention. Silence created uneasiness even amidst the luxury of the modern facilities, room heated by steam and the temperature controlled to personal comfort irrespective of the snow storm outside. Her mood was desperate and the situation needed to be handled with finesse. They contemplated strategic approach that would be appropriate to pacify her agitated state.

"I am fully in agreement with your predicament. Anyone in your place would have revolted. You had great expectation and the experience has been contrary. You feel that the dreams have been shattered. It is natural. We however need to appreciate that life is not all roses and only by crossing the barriers, travelling along the thorn laden path that we get unsullied pleasure." Kamal calmly stated.

"In life there is nothing worse than the feeling that no one cares whether you exist, no one bothers as to what you want, what you have to say and there is an eternal conflict at the heart of human existence: our desires and fulfillment as we face life. Our awareness of world's harsh realities, injustice is agonizing; but we have to face. The show must go on. And I believe, we have to find a new door, a new approach, not out of pride or arrogance but simply because the existing things do not seem fit into the life." Vidya paused and continued, "God knows that we are all artists of life. One day He gives a chisel and hammer to carve out a sculpture and another day paints and brush to make a painting. And we should look forward to build a future, leaving our pains behind."

She did not respond instantly. After a moments thought, she mentioned, "I am passing through a phase when life has been overwhelmed by terrible tumult and oppressions. I thought of sharing with you and get some direction."

It was not such an easy task. The scope was limited to a bit of consolation and counseling. Kamal tried to think it over. Vidya could feel the sensitiveness and requested her husband, "I think you are feeling sleepy. Please go to bed. We'll take a few more minutes. It's already late."

The next morning when Kamal awoke, Saraswathi was ready for leaving after breakfast. While leaving she thanked them for the hospitality. They bade good bye, "Pray all well. Take care and keep in touch" Vidya said and hugged.

"She seems more composed than the previous evening, I think." Kamal mentioned his wife.

"She is so sweet. God certainly would show her a new path of life." Vidya replied and got into her normal routine.

The office opened after the New Year and usual activity followed. While interacting with local officials, he broached in the subject of family discord and obtained details of the officers concerned with social counselling. Though he was not acquainted with them, nor it was within the scope of his official duties, in order to ascertain the possibility of their help in the matter of Saraswathi's problem, he met and discussed without providing any specific details. The response was encouraging. He surmised, 'an ounce of help in need is more than a ton of sympathy at heart' and proceeded. He located the responsible officer, offered all details with the condition of anonymity. The officer was more than helpful. He called Herr Schneider informally and explained his responsibilities for his wife, who happened to be an expatriate. He also admonished him of dire consequences in the event of complaint.

Time passed. Their meeting, his initiatives were relegated to the background against the dictates of duty. And by the end of school session, they were to return back. Another officer has also joined to take over the assignment.

In order to introduce the new officer and also to thank all those who supported him in the course of his tenure, he planned a formal dinner. While deciding the guests, his wife asked if Saraswathi could be invited along with her husband.

"It's just no problem. The weather is fine and they could easily return. I'll ask Yuvanhoe to call her and send an invitation." He confirmed.

Both of them arrived early with a bouquet and a bottle of champagne. They wanted to personally thank Mr. and Mrs. Kamal for their help. Yuvanhoe also arrived with the favourite chocolates for the children and said, "Madam, I am taking charge and you may please relax a bit before the guests arrive."

"Thanks, Yuvanhoe. Today Saraswathi will also help you."

Yuvanhoe tried to correct in a lighter vein, "Madam, she is no longer Saraswathi. She is Frau Sarah Schneider and a German citizen."

And Kamal interject, "Okay, she is Sarah *alias* Saraswathi."

Other guests arrived. Drinks, dinner followed. Spacially selected light Indian music regaled the guests. The last official dinner at his residence was over to everyone's satisfaction. All left, some extending invitation and others promising to meet again. Saraswathi too left; for she came with her husband. Children repaired to their respective bed. Vidya busied to arrange food items and Kamal helped with dishwasher. An unusual hush permeated replacing hour long hustle and bustle.

"I am at your service, madam" Kamal cajoled, breaking silence.

"You better take rest. I'll take care of the rest." was a quick reply. He left smiling.

After a while she came, changed her dress and informed, "She was feeling grateful to you for your intervention because of which her life has changed."

"Well yes, you too pursued her to change the perspective of her life. You know relationship is a two way traffic." He continued philosophically, "In any case, it gives us immense pleasure to see her happy; Saraswathi *alias* Sarah!"

In everybody's life, at some time, the inner fire goes out. We should all be thankful for those people who rekindle the inner spirit.

– Albert Schweitzer

6

An Encounter with Robbers

Man thinks that he is the doer, but it's a mistake.
It is HE who does every thing and he is a tool.

—Ramana Maharshi

Events, incidents, experiences pleasant and not so pleasant spice life. And generally, moments of agony and ecstasy tend to merge in the time horizon leaving only reminiscences. One such reminiscence is my story, an encounter with robbers in the train four decades ago. It is borrowed from the eidetic memory that captivated my mind for quite some time.

It was third week of December 1966 and must have been a Wednesday because the dining hall of 'Vishwakarma Hostel' in Benaras Hinhu University was unusually crowded early in the evening as every one of us was eager to finish dinner and occupy a cosy seat to enjoy Ceylon's year ending Vividh Bharathi programme.

I took the opportunity to inform and know if any one else would be interested to go home during the year end and mentioned, "Friends, I plan to visit home during this X-mas. Anyone interested should be ready early Friday evening to leave for the station after dinner."

"I was also thinking to go home for a few days." Ananta replied immediately.

"Are you sure? Your father may not approve of your visit."

"I have already written to him and he wanted me to come with other friends and not alone."

"Well, then I shall have your company."

"You normally preferred to stay and relax during short vacations. Is anything urgent that calls for this visit in the final year?" asked Prasanta.

"I feel a bit homesick; as you know I could not go home during puja holidays." I replied.

On Friday evening the four of us, Ananta, Brajendra, Subudhi and myself took dinner and left for the station on two rickshaws. Manik joined us at the railway station.

In those days there was no direct train to Orissa from Benaras and we had to travel via Howrah. Normally we tried to reach Howrah by noon and preferred to avail of the most convenient connecting train for onward journey. from Howrah at 1430 hrs.

Our journey to Howrah was enjoyable beyond expectation with berths for all of us in Kalka Mail. We had lunch at the station and boarded East Coast Express scheduled to depart at 1430 hrs. Initially the train was not so crowed and we occupied a long wooden plank in a general unreserved compartment for five of us. We put our bags and blazers on the over head space and spent time scanning a few magazines we carried along. A Bengali family occupied the opposite side.

It was about 1700 hrs. The cacophony of a bevy of vendors, wanderers, beggars, passengers, their relatives and friends on the longest platform reminded us of Kharagpur station. The crowded compartment that mingled a melody of its own moments earlier gradually reduced along with train's speed. Most of the passengers alighted, some reached their destination, a few to change for other trains, many for buying, refreshing and the remaining to roam around to peep in other compartments to enjoy what they described 'a feast for the eyes'. Our compartment became deserted with exception of a few like me remaining inside as the custodian of the belongings. I knew from previous experience that the train would stop for at least half an hour and I sat at the window vainly busy with a small radio receiver to tune to the Calcutta channel for some music.

I overheard a gentleman passing by and perhaps trying to caution, "Please be careful. Some miscreants have entered your compartment."

"We do not have valuables except our clothing, why worry?" I thought and ignored.

It was around 1730 hrs the train whistled to signal its departure and those who were to continue their journey rushed in. The sun set and the light dimmed. Darkness spread its wings. A few bulbs flickered on inside the compartment. Ananta came with some bananas and sat along side me. Subudhi was chitchatting in the adjacent area. Brajendra and Manik were not in sight. The train moved rhythmically piercing the engulfed darkness around. An unusual quiet prevailed as commuters seemed busy with themselves. While we were discussing our expected arrival at Balasore and the further bus connection for home, a gentleman rushed in and said not addressing in particular, "Your friend is in trouble. Please help him."

Perplexed we looked each other, both of us thinking "Is the message for us?"

No sooner we heard Subudhi's agonized shrill, rushed to the other side Ananta following. To my surprise there was no passenger in the area occupied by about eight persons, except Subudhi and a well built person bending over him. He had assaulted him with a severe punch on his forehead that ruptured the skin with blood visible in the dim light. For a split second I found it hard even to cry for help. Filled with agonizing frustration of powerlessness in the face of imminent disaster, I rushed close to Subudhi trying to obstruct the fiend from further assault. Instantly I heard a thud and turned to realize that Ananta collapsed and writhed on the other wooden plank dazed and stunned, hit by another person of the gang.

Though we have been travelling in that route for four years we have never faced any untoward incident like this. Though helpless, I could not help standing as mute witness and let the situation unfret without trying to do something and I almost shouted in high pitch,

"Why are you beating him? What has he done to you? We are students from University and going home. We are innocent."

And then I begged, "Please stop."

The person withdrew and moved back a bit. I felt reprieved. I was about to touch Subudhi's head to wipe out blood with my handkerchief, he pulled me away and showed a knife that glittered even in the dim light. I also noticed two more bandits each holding a knife and fiercely eyeing the passengers. The compartment packed to capacity, filled with great bustle assayed pin drop silence. Everyone, without exception perhaps was terror-struck for any discussion or action. Instinctively, I got so carried away that there was hardly any time for me to think and be frightened. Time stopped. A second was stilled to infinity. And in that brief timeless lacuna, my mind was drained free of tension and fear. It was as if I were detached from the past and future, aware simultaneously of the self and the adversaries and muster as much courage as I could. The pent up anger, frustration led me to the final release of strength and I tightly gripped his right fore arm that held the knife with my two hands.

"Please don't do this. I have already told you we are students and have no enmity with you. Please forgive if there has been any misunderstanding." I tried to explain.

Quite contrary to the expectation that my blabbing - a dialogue of the deaf, he folded the knife, put in his pocket and sat down on Subudhi's side. Trying to mask my abomination and provide a buffer for my friend, I squeezed in between them and waited for his reaction.

"He is responsible for my loss. Why did he interfere?" was his immediate reproach.

"What loss? Has my friend taken something from you? Please tell me. I'll get for you, I promise."

"No, he has not taken anything. But he interfered and the rascal has escaped with my money. It is Rs.42,000/- (It was a big money in those days.) and that thief has taken and vanished with my bag."

I found it too difficult to comprehend the scenario. Though I knew Subudhi would make things clear, strategically I kept him isolated. He was in deep remorse, sobbing with pain and puerile tears rolling down his cheek. And in an effort to divert his attention, I proposed,

"Let us search for him. He cannot escape from the moving train."

He truculently nodded and bent down to search if he was hiding below the seat. I was mired to follow despite the obnoxious smell of some country liquor from him. After a brief search in vain, he reproved my friend and asked with asperity to learn not to interfere with others' affairs. I opted not to altercate but consent his obdurate remark. He looked around again and repeated his warning with stern atrocity. The train slowed a bit and the gang of five men quickly jumped down the platform. It was 'Nekursani' a small station as we read from the signboard.

I desperately needed someone to talk to and searched for Ananta. He too was missing from the scene. Within moments many people came around, some inquiring the damage, others counseling against my friend's misadventure and a few asking that first aid need to be provided. Ananta also appeared and informed me that while we were searching for the person he got up and was pulling the chain to stop the train, but nothing happened. So far it never occurred to me that we could pull the chain in a moment of despair to attract attention of the authority. We both pulled the chain again for first aid from the train guard, but yet again the train did not stop.

Though I wanted to hear from Subudhi why all this happened, the circumstance demanded our attention to focus on what need to be done in the instant situation. We saw that there was swelling on his forehead and the blood had clotted. Commiseration, exclamation and bizarre to realty discussions emerged, it was rather difficult for us to participate as anguish, helplessness, frustration, injustice engulfed. One passenger informed that the train would stop at Jaleshwar after about ten minutes. The station being in Orissa, we expected some definite help and waited almost in silence for the time to pass.

The train came to halt after a long wait and immediately we ran to the guard to ask why the train did not stop when the chain was pulled in emergency and get first aid. As luck would have it, we got nothing. On persistent demand from a crowd of passengers the guard went to the station master to telephone the next station to arrange for first aid. We all returned as the train whistled to move on. Brajendra and Manik also returned. Learning about the mishap, they felt pity being away in the hour of need.

The journey would be an hour to reach the next stop, we were told. Realising that we owe a clarification on the circumstance that led to such uncontrollable mess, Subudhi intoned,

"I started talking with a boy who happened to be from my place and working for a firm in Orissa and its head office.is at Calcutta. That devil joined at Kharagpur and sat next to the boy. A few minutes after the train left, he suddenly, without any reason or rhyme started slapping the boy. I did ask him to stop and threatened to pull the chain and shout for help. An altercation between us ensued. In the mean time he found the boy missing and in a violent animal rage he charged me for helping the rascal run away with his money."

He paused and concluded, "I really don't know beyond this."

An elderly gentleman intervened, "Let me explain. The boy is a messenger carrying about Rs. 40,000 from the firm's head office to site. He withdrew the amount from a bank in Calcutta and being followed since then. There are a few gangs who operate in this 'Dantan-Nekarsani' zone and rob. It is organized crime perpetrated by professional groups in train, bus including cars. They have informers to visit strategic places in the city and tip off."

The group gathered listened with avidity and he continued,

"I really appreciate the way you managed an air of sangfroid in the midst of crisis. Your defiance and flippant multi lingual appeal perhaps disarmed them. Actually they live by rapine and violence. Long exposure to a life of errors and vices has obscured their intellect. It is strange indeed that they left without the booty."

"Where is the boy?" some one asked.

"We put him below the sitting benches camouflaged with luggage. He must be up by now.'

The boy came and confirmed that he withdrew Rs. 42,000 from a bank that day and carrying to the firm for salary distribution. He regretted that Subudhi was assaulted for him.

The train stopped at Balasore. A paramedic came for first aid to the compartment. We along with the guard went to the station master to report the encounter and lodged a FIR. While four of us were to get down at this station Subudhi was to travel another four hours. We requested him to join us and rest for the night, but he was in no mood to delay his arrival as his parents would be anxious. We solicited co-passengers favour to take care of him during the journey.

We wished him a fine journey ahead and waved till he was out of sight. The experience was so unpleasant for all of us that we mentally resolved not to travel that stretch during night.

7

Unforgettable Moments

The heart wants what it wants...
There's no logic to those things. —*Woody Allen*

The sprawling lush green lawns with colourful winter flowers like dahlia, pansy, marigold on the either side of rajpath offer picturesque sight for nature lovers. The officers and officials of the central secretariat wait to come out of the buildings during the lunch hour in groups for a walk in the sun, stand and discuss office, national and international issues with peanuts/fruits or look around the vendors offer on 'sale' a variety of items.

December this year has been very severe. A cold wave condition has prevailed for some time with biting but fitful wind scouring the city in spite of the clear sky. Some preferred to stay inside and others who ventured to follow routine could not put up with the chill and had to come back. They searched for a room with sunshine to continue their lunch time gossip.

Mr. Satya Prakash preferred to stay inside. He was basking in the sun and flipping through a magazine. The telephone rang, and he responded,

"Hello"

"Hope you are not terribly occupied. As no one is around today, December fever you know, I want to share your sunshine. It wouldn't be free, of course. I have a sample packet of peanuts." went on his colleague Mr. Saran.

"You are we welcome without samples. Please do come, I am waiting."

Mr. Satya Prakash was an officer in the ministry of Industry and Commerce. He enjoyed high respect in the bureaucratic circle as an intelligent, knowledgeable officer and model of efficiency. He was 'S.P.' to peers and seniors, and 'Sir' to junior officers and the staff. His room in Udyog Bhawan was well furnished with added advantage of the window facing south. And as a result the room has been endowed with rich sunshine during winter. The brilliant sunshine on his sofa as against out side chill attracted him to stay in and scan through some magazines.

Mr. Saran came with a packet, put it on the small centre table and started to open. Mr. Prakash spread an old news paper on the table to avoid dirt on the floor and they sat down comfortably. While Mr. Saran mentioned how envious he was of the so nicely maintained room, he also explained what made him buy the packet on way to office and quickly proceeded to do justice to the peanuts.

Mr. Prakash too held a piece of peanut and as he tried to split open his mind was catapulted down the memory lane. The reminiscence of one of those unforgettable moments appeared fresh in his mind like paintings on a broad canvas.

He along with his wife and children used to enjoy peanuts at home during winter times. Sarala was very fond of roasted peanuts and all other members of the family used to join her for company. She used to take care of the splitting, cleaning of the peanuts and passed on to the children and her husband. She always enjoyed feeding the family and very happy with her limited share. She lived true to her name, perhaps only for other's pleasure. On one occasion, she had a limited few and when Satya asked for some, she enjoined,

"Please try to separate some and eat, you are no more a child."

"Well, you know how dependent I am."

"You always use sweet words to fool me."

"Is it necessary?" he quipped.

"What? What?"

"Well, well...I was just trying to explain."

"See, how your father teases me"

The children burst in to laughter and she smiled again.

The scene stirred deep in his heart. He became emotional at the very thought of her innocence that has left an indelible imprint. Trying to battle back tears, he reflected,

She was beautiful as the moon in the horizon, graceful as the cypress that sways in the night wind and glisten in the sheen of the stars. While the moon looks down and reflects but only one moon, she reflected a smile that smote all hearts to love.

He wanted to live with the secret happiness of the sweet excitement of the memory of her touch, warmth of her embrace, the glow of heaven in her eyes and the tenderness of her heart...

In the mean time another two colleagues have entered the room to join in the group and share the cosy sunshine. They were apoplectic to meet Mr. Prakash with tears rolling down the cheeks. They all along had an impression about him as a very stern, disciplined officer and a strong hearted person.

Mr. Prakash welcomed them with controlled emotion and offered them seat with invitation to join for tasting the peanuts, courtesy Mr. Saran. The circumstances, no doubt wafted away his feelings from the surface; but deep inside he thought,

It was but yesterday we met in a dream. You have sung to me in my aloneness and I, of our longings vowed to build a tower in the sky.

Years have passed by but for him time seemed to be standing still. He was not sure with whom he would share how their dream has collapsed and she was no more. It was an easy platitude to say that the dead lived in the memory of the living, but what substitute was memory for the loving voice and the strong enclosing arms that he longed. And he fancied,

"If in the twilight of the memory we met once more, you shall sing to me a deeper song and I promise we shall build another tower in the sky."

He however assured mentally that what ever be the weather those moments would remain sunlit in his memory to lighten his heart and change the tragedy of the ignorant world into a 'Divine comedy of joy.'

The reverie came to an end with the sound of tapping on the door and the orderly requesting permission if tea could be served.

8

Kitchen Blues

Let me not pray to be sheltered against dangers, but to be fearless in facing them.

—Rabindra Nath Tagore

Kavita and Manoj are a young working couple in a metro city. Kavita, on completion of her management programme in a premiere B-school is working as an executive in a multinational corporation and Manoj operates his stock broking firm. While Manoj is attuned to the metro life, Kavita is in search of accommodation which has open space and located in a serene environment. She still remembers her young days spent in a small town in a spacious house located amidst sprawling lawns, scattered trees in a tropical pleasance.

After marriage Manoj had selected so many houses which they visited, but she did not like any of them. Kavita had a mental image of how her home should be and all the flats they had looked failed to impress her. Both Kavita and Manoj wanted to live near the office so that the time for commutation could be shortened and they could have more time for each other. This limited the area where they could search for accommodation. Kavita had almost lost hope of finding a suitable flat and was about to make a compromise.

A chance meeting with Mr. Gupta, a family friend whom she barely remembered gave her some hope. Mr Gupta informed that he had a small bungalow and was looking for a tenant and would be more than happy if it fulfilled their requirement. The following weekend they visited the house. Kavita was in love with its architecture and ambience. The house was not only Vaastu perfect, it was also very spacious, fully furnished, and had a car park and a beautiful garden. It was adjacent to a big park and other amenities were nearby. The greenery and cool breeze won her heart. It was the physical manifestation of her dream house.

Twenty-eight year old Manoj could feel the excitement of twenty-five year old Kavita to shift and decorate the home as per her plan. It was the same excitement that attracted him towards her. He had met her in her office in a hot summer day last year. He had come to meet her for official purposes and just could not stop admiring her looks, leadership qualities and confidence. Her doe-eyes, long ebony straight hair and perfect body made him skip a heart beat. He met her a few times on minor issues and soon Kavita sensed that he wanted to be more than just a business friend. He forever seemed to be trying to find excuses to meet her. As for Manoj, he was overawed and smitten by Kavita. He loved the way she handled such stressful matters and her genuine concern and caring nature made him fall in love with her. He laughs when she reminds him how awkwardly he had stared at her. They courted for two months and with the blessings of both their parents, married on the auspious occasion of Shivratri. Manoj and Kavita were great worshippers of Lord Shivji and they believed marriage on Shivratri was a good omen.

Prior to shifting they decided to clean and paint the house. The job was entrusted to Shyam whom they happen to know. "OK...Madam. Tomorrow ...I will start tomorrow," stammered Shyam. He had a stutter, but an able worker. Shyam was a jack-of-all-trades, who made his living by doing the odd jobs in the locality. A day before Diwali, he finished distempering of the whole house and Kavita was happy with the new look. "It looks so perfect," she said. "It's now ready for the *griha-pravesh* ceremony the day after Diwali."

Next morning on the auscipous day of Diwali she surveyed the house before the *griha-pravesh* ceremony. She noticed palm imprints on the kitchen walls and was stunned. She had an uneasy feeling and wondered how it could happen.

"It is a bad omen," Kavita told Manoj as she showed him the hand imprints. "Kavita dear, Shyam might not have painted it. Don't worry we'll call him again." He tried to console her.

"But I saw him painting myself, I supervised it," argued Kavita.

"Maybe Shyam accidentally put his palm. You know how they work now-a-days. We shall ask Shyam to come and re-do it again."

"OK, " replied Kavita lost in thought "I'll call him."

But Kavita had an unnerving experience. She did not call Shyam but dialed another phone number.

"Hello, I am Kavita, may I speak to Mr.Gupta,"

"Yes, Kavita beti, How are you?"

"Fine Uncle, Happy Diwali."

"Happy Diwali to both of you."

"Uncle there is something I want to show you, could you come immediately please."

"Is everything all right, Kavita?"

"Yes Uncle, everything is fine. Please come. We are waiting for you."

Mr. Gupta lived close by. He arrived within few minutes. Kavita told Mr. Gupta about the whole palm imprint episode in brief.

Mr. Gupta reluctantly unfolded the hidden reality. "Kavita, this bunglow was a wedding gift from us to my son and daughter-in-law. They came to this house two days before Diwali. And on the day of Diwali my son and daughter-in-law mysteriously died."

Kavita was listening intensely. And the word "died" echoed in her mind and for few seconds, she was motionless, her face giving a sense of fear, and her body suddenly started shivering, the sight of the strange palm imprints appeared in the mind and she froze once again.

She persuaded Manoj to continue with the present accommodation and not take the risk of occupying Mr. Gupta's house. Manoj tried to convince her that it was mere superstition and that she should forget the episode. But Kavita was too terrified to listen.

9

A Letter for You

Amid the work of darker powers, She is here
To heal the evils and mistakes of space,
And change the tragedy of the ignorant world
Into a Divine Comedy of Joy. —*Sri Aurobindo*

There are times in ones life when one is at a cross road. Sitakanta faced such a situation after retirement from the Government service in Delhi. He had all the facilities for living in Delhi; he owned a flat in a posh colony, had membership of a club and a number of close friends. The ancestral home in the village also offered all facilities for living along with near and dear ones. He however has lived life as a loner in the crowd. Now, with declining age he had to decide whether he could continue to lead a similar life all alone. The dilemma continued for some time.

Life is but a bundle of dilemmas. And these need to be resolved. Sitakanta with his experience, intuition and full appreciation of the present decided to finally settle at Bishnupur – the district headquarters of his ancestral village. He rented a small flat as a transit place to find an accommodation of his choice.

It was a unique spring afternoon, though unusual to the coastal region and Sitakanta was busy in arranging the paraphernalia he transported. The bell rang. When he opened the door, he found a cute little girl standing in front.

"Mother says a letter for you, sir." she chortled extending her hand from a distance with a letter.

"Thank you and what is your name?" he asked.

"Vasudha" she replied.

"Please come in." requested Sitakanta and went inside to find something for her.

By the time he returned with a toffee, she was gone.

Standing at the half opened door, Sitakanta felt he has travelled a time tunnel and was back to more than three decades. The event mirrored fresh as it were only yesterday.

It was vacation time and I was busy preparing for the Administrative Services. My aunt happened to visit and found that the place was crowded for me to concentrate in studies. She invited me to come along with her to her place which normally remained unoccupied. She explained that it would be good for me to study without disturbance and that she would enjoy my company for some time at least.

I reached the small town from the village atmosphere. The house was a two storey building with two rooms in the first floor which remained vacant. The whole floor was left at my disposal.

I found it most suitable for my study. And I realised aunty was not only strict in timing for food and sleep but also for rest and recreation. Though her scheduled for meal was direct lunch at about 1130 hrs, afternoon tea at 1600 hrs and dinner at 2030 hrs, she told me that I should take fruits and biscuits at intervals because good food is essential for concentration. She also informed that she would prepare morning breakfast at 0630 hrs prior to her morning rituals. The schedule continued as it was quite acceptable to me as well.

After tea in the afternoon, I used to spend some time in the open terrace to enjoy the nature around and get some free space. There was a big bunglow on the opposite side of the road. It was a three storied building, the first floor and second floor with reduced covered area and leaving open terrace and veranda. In few days I noticed that a sweet little girl would come to the terrace that was in the same level with that of mine, wait for some time and again go inside. I continued to watch her for quite some time thinking that she probably had a similar strict timing for afternoon snacks after the school.

As the vacation was closing by, I got busier with studies. The routine continued and I couldn't but notice the girl coming, waiting for some time in the veranda and then going inside after a while. Though I knew that aunty was a widow, spending a very lonely life with limited acquaintance, one day during tea I ventured to ask, "Aunty, do you know the family living in the bunglow on the opposite side of the road, a few houses off?"

"Why, what is the matter?" she queried.

"Nothing special...but I notice the big bunglow is unusually quiet."

"Well, there used to be lot of activities in the big house. It is about a year since the family suffered a

severe accident and everything has come to stand still as I learnt from one of the servants."

The unresolved mystery captivated me as I had no other means to probe further. A few days passed. On one afternoon after I spent some time on the terrace, came to my room and about to sit down for studies, there was knock on the door. I came out and astonished to see the pretty little girl on the terrace of the bunglow stood before me. She handed me an open inland letter saying, "A letter for you!"

"Thank you." I said. As I stood aghast to figure out how a letter for me could reach her, she said calmly and clearly, "You are also expecting a letter from your mother and you can read this."

By the time I could regain my composure I found she was gone.

It was a letter her mother had written to her some time back with a dose of explanation and urgency for being away, consolation and advice to be good and above all promise to return soon. And I went on thinking why did she give it to me. During dinner I discussed the matter with my aunty and she told me that she would get it checked up. The whole night I could not sleep properly as there was no way to get into the mystery. Her mellifluous voice played over and over again in my head. I woke up early and decided to pay a visit and clear the cobweb.

The stars faded and in their place was soft crimson glow in the eastern horizon heralding the imminent sun rise. The night breeze has quietened. Incessant chatter of the song birds could now be heard. I paced, waited and with the sun rise walked across the street with mind laden with questions. The heavy wrought iron gate of the bunglow was closed. The area looked spacious but the surrounding wanting. A sepulchral stillness hung around. Curtains of a few first floor rooms ballooned gently out. A heavy built man with grey hair and moustache, fresh from bath and tilak on fore head appeared. He ushered me to a chair, "Please sit. Hope you have not waited long. I was busy with my rituals."

Before I could explain the purpose of my visit, he continued talking that reflected fiercely possessive of his respectability trying to cling to the old morality. He had all praise for the comforting certainties of his young days and also of serving the mansion for over four decades. Though I started feeling a bit impatient, I allowed expressing his feelings.

Finally I opened the letter received from the young girl and before I opened my mouth, he said with a tone charged with emotion and eyes filled, "I know. I know... She told me that you too are anxious and eagerly awaiting a letter."

"But I have never met her. And she is too young to bother about unknown person like me." I said.

"She told me that you also wait for the postman every afternoon as she has been waiting."

"Well, I am new to this place and have been staying with my aunty for some time to prepare for my examination. I don't know any body here. I just look around and relax in the afternoon for some time after tea. And I have seen her coming to the veranda around that time. " I explained.

"She has also noted you and innocently thought that you are in the similar situation."

"Could you kindly elaborate? It difficult for me to comprehend."

He explained me in detail the sad demise of her parents in an accident about ten month back. "Presently her Uncle is here to oversee the business. Though she knows about her father's death, she has been told that her mother is away to take care of the business affairs that need to be attended to urgently."

He paused and then continued, "The letter you have was posted by me to assuage her desire to meet her mother. But for how long?"

I could not find words to express my feelings. I sat speechless. Though I came to return the letter I instantly felt it would not be proper and hurt her. Before leaving I thanked him for his cordiality and asked his name.

"Here everybody calls me 'Pandeji', you may adopt."

I thanked again and promised to meet him before leaving for home. As I stood up and turned, I saw the cute little girl standing at the far end of the veranda in her night dress. Her innocuous natural smile created tiny fissures in her smooth pink cheeks. She looked exquisite as an ineffable quintessential angel direct from heaven. Adorable! I realised she, like the mother earth could feel what others couldn't. And that was her greatness.

I walked slowly. I turned back and saw that she was still standing there looking at me. I found it difficult to take my eyes off. I had an overwhelming experience: 'nearly all the world's poetry in the transitoriness of life, love and beauty the knowledge that time's winged chariot have knives in its wheels.'

Moments passed by. Sitakanta stood transfixed. The sound of the horn informing the arrival of Mr. Purohit, the house owner brought him to the present state. He reflected. "The memories are forever a source of great happiness."

10

A Friend Indeed!

Far and away he best prize that life offers is
the chance to work hard at work worth doing.

—Theodore Roosevelt

It was late April in 1990. Delhites have started feeling the heat of early summer. Noon approaching, the blue sky has turned white with blinding sun overhead. Hot wind, though not in its usual fury, has started blowing. And Akash was returning home from his friends with whom he has spent the morning in gossip. He was in a hurry to reach before noon and avoid mother's sermon and reprimand.

Akash has stepped into the teenage, a period of dreamy adolescence. He lived in a hutment colony in trans-Yamuna with his mother, who is the bread earner. He left going to school a few years ago despite his mother's pursuance to do something useful. He however despised living under poverty, scarcity and wanted to be a person with huge wealth to buy all luxury of the world. In the process, he had acquired friends in the neighbouring area, who fuelled his aspiration and even induced him to the path of small crimes for adventure and pleasure.

While turning to the lane that leads to his hut, he noticed that a group of four boys were mercilessly beating a frail boy who was begging in trepidation. He stopped, went closer and felt pity. He asked, "Why are you beating him?"

"Ask him. He deserves to be kicked." was a terse reply.

"But it's unequal."

"He foiled our bid to get our booty."

"Oh, you wanted to snatch from him."

"What has this poor fella to offer?"

"I would suggest you to leave him. He may die in this heat and you all will be hanged." He cautioned.

"If you have so much sympathy, please take him along."

"I'll do that." His tone insolent.

They eyed both sternly and left with warning, "If you come on our way again, we wouldn't leave you."

Akash started to walk away, but the boy followed to thank him. And out of curiosity, he asked, "Why are they so furious?"

"They were snatching a bag from a passer by. I diverted their attention saying, 'be careful, some one is coming' and as they looked afar, the man ran away."

"You seem to be very intelligent. Where do you stay?"

"No home. All alone in life." He replied almost weeping.

"Well, I have forgotten to ask your name. And what do you do?"

"I am Akshyay. Do some odd jobs and feed to survive."

By the time they reached the hutment where Akash lived. He invited him, "Come with me to our place. Mother must have cooked something. We shall share."

"How can I take your share?"

"My mother is very compassionate. She'll arrange."

They went inside. And Akshyay touched his mother's feet and stood in supplication.

"Mom, he is Akshyay. He was being beaten by some boys and I called him."

"He should go to home. His parents must be waiting for him" his mother admonished.

"I have nobody, maa." He said fighting tears.

She found the boy starving and said, "Okay. Both of you wash up and have some chapatti."

They ate and sat down. His mother enquired about his work, living and out of kindness offered him to live with them. "I cannot be a burden to you." He was apologetic.

His reply overwhelmed her and she thought that the boy would certainly be of help to change the attitude of his son. She promised, "We shall look for some work for you and also some education."

In the course of few days, she took him along to 'Baba', an old man who used to teach orphans in his ashram which she visited some times for solace. It was situated in the neighbouring town of U P and Akshyay became a regular student. Baba found him a devoted disciple having inclination to pursue the path of spirituality. He learnt of his past and also his sincerity to work hard towards wellness of the society. He was in need of someone who would continue with the tradition and accepted him.

Akshyay's visit to Akash and his mother gradually reduced. On one occasion when he reached with some vegetables grown in the ashram and searched for Akash, his mother expressed her anxieties and requested him to pursue his son to do something useful. He promised to do his best but failed to bring any change in Akash. He only lamented, for he could not do anything for a friend and brother who has been instrumental for his settlement.

Time passed. As success succeeded success, Akshyay grew in an environment of discipline following a path shown by his guru. He became Yogi Akshyayanand taking charge of the ashram and developed it to a centre for Yoga along with a 'Balashram' for rehabilitation of orphans. The institution assumed the status of a model for society.

On the other hand, Akash started living alone, as his mother left Delhi along with her employer who retired and offered her job at his home in Rajasthan. As a sincere and concerned mother, her life revolved round her sibling and she expected his son to earn a good living which she would be proud of. But as luck would have it, she found the only son wayward and uncontrollable. She saw her life stretching ahead like an endless, bleak and intolerable road. Faced with agonizing frustration of helplessness in the face of imminent doom, she painfully accepted the offer. She considered it a better option rather than everyday bickering and thought that his solitary life might respond to wisdom. She left the key and her address with a trusted neighbour hoping her motherly love would one day rekindle his spirit.

As she longed for her son to return, he grew up, unrestraint with his over enthusiasm to satiate sensory pleasures by any means. Bad friends fanned his passion and his petty crimes increased in all dimensions. He was donned as 'Bhai' and became one of the 'wanted' in the police record.

* * *

It was mid March of 2005. Holi has just passed. Severe cold of north India's winter declined and summer yet to take on. A pleasant evening during the brief transition. The inmates of 'Balashram' completed their usual prayer and were going to their rooms. The night sky had a few stars. Usual calm hung except the hushed tone of some young ones. Sudden rush of foot steps disturbed silence of the ashram. A man came running, chased by two policemen one after another, all armed with revolvers. And the man took a kid as hostage to bargain his escape.

Yogi Akshyayanand appeared in the scene. He walked to the police and begged, "Please, please do me a favour. Do drop the guns. It's a holy place. I'll talk to him."

"He is a hard criminal and dangerous. Please don't interfere." The police inspector warned.

Yogi sensed the mood of the police personnel and contacted the DCP who happened to be a regular visitor of the Yoga classes on Sundays. He explained him the position and requested for his instruction to the police officer and handed over the cell phone to the police inspector, who talked to DCP and in a moment the police officer said politely, “We are waiting outside. Please do call if you need us and remember he is too dangerous.”

The policemen left the site. Yogi walked to the man holding the child. He exuded calm and peace. And even in the dim light, he instantly recognised that the person was none other than his one time friend and saviour, Akash. His unexpected change saddened him to the core. Controlling emotion, he spoke, “Mere Bhai, Akash. Please come with me. The police have gone away. I have been longing to meet you and maa.”

His soothing voice, pious zeal and open headed munificence disarmed him. He too recognised that he was Akshyay. He dropped the gun and released the child. They hugged closely and his loving touch melted away the animal in him.

The Yogi instructed one of his assistants, “Please take the kids to their rooms. Do direct DCP to the office, when he arrives. And leave us alone for a few minutes.”

All present, his assistants and the kids seemed baffled. To enliven the environ someone remarked, “Please disperse. It was a film shooting and it’s over.”

Akshyay sat close to his friend and asked, “Police accuses of grave charges against you. I hope it is untrue.”

He cried and cried without answering. Both sat quiet for some time and Akash confessed, “It’s true and I am ashamed of my actions. It’s the result of my uncompromising ambition, greed to become rich overnight and possess all the luxuries of the world. I am so unfortunate that mother also left me. I am a sinner."

And he went on crying ceaselessly. Akshyay wanted him to cleanse and therefore left him alone and walked out. He saw DCP approaching and went ahead to greet him,

"Good evening sir. My apologies for disturbing you. He is inside, alone and repenting for his sins."

He paused and continued, "I'll not interfere with your process. My only request is; please give him a chance to change. I am prepared to offer guarantee that he will henceforth tread the path of peace. He is my responsibility."

DCP stood still and thought over the proposition. He has seen the yogi to be a very conscientious and pious man. And so far the inident has not gone on record that he has been caught. He could take a chance and kill two birds at one shot: an offering to the yogi who has helped his wife to come out of depression and initiate a novel experiment, which may prove to be an eye opener to the society.

"Since you are prepared to take charge, I am inclined to agree with your proposal" he confirmed.

"I am grateful. I don't know how to thank you for your decision. I confirm, I'll strive to do my best to transform him to your satisfaction." He submitted.

DCP wished him 'good luck' and left briskly.

After a few moments, he arranged some refreshment and sat down in front of Akash. He said,

"Have something and I'll show you a room for your stay. The police have left, but may be waiting for you outside our premises. You have to be careful. Please do stay here a few days. Don't leave. And you have to be ready for dinner in an hour. We all sit and eat together."

The night passed. Akshyay designed a plan for him for a few days; to follow the strict schedule of the ashram essential for his concentration and ask one of his assistants to report. As usual he woke up when the stars still twinkled in the sky. He completed his morning rituals and entered Akash's room to signal a new dawn of his life. He found him sleepless, but did not question. 'He needs time to accept the change' he thought.

"Good morning. Hope you are comfortable. Let's make a new beginning, a new life. Forget the past. Cleanse the mind like a teacher cleans a blackboard for new lesson. And follow the routine of the ashram a few days." He advised.

He listened and said, "I am prepared to follow a new path. Please promise, you will get my mother."

"I promise." He said and embraced to inspire confidence.

The next few days were difficult for him to follow a strict routine life. But he tried and soon adjusted himself. Akshyay only met him during prayer, lunch and dinner and encouraged him. His assistants helped and reported encouraging development. In the moments of loneliness, Akash became pensive thinking of the past that haunted him like a shadow. While discussing about the future with one inmate of the ashram, he expressed, "Yogi Akshyayanandji is so nice. He is working out a plan for my rehabilitation. He has advised me to accept the failures and open a new door, attempt the impossible, while others may laugh or criticize. I'll not let him down."

About a month passed. He seemed inured to the life of a ashramite without any complaints. On a few occasions, he has also expressed his desire to do something to eke out a living. Akshyay felt satisfied and relieved that his friend was on the path of true transformation. He consulted some of the known businessmen of the area. Almost all advised that there was a need for a service provider to compressively take care of the needs of a marriage. He thought of the project that would cater to all section of the society and got it vetted by some business experts. When he informed him of the details including a location and tie up with associated service providers' willingness to participate in the venture, Akash was instantly excited, but skeptical, "I swear, I'll honestly try my best. But will people trust me when they learn about my background?"

"Stop being what you were; become what you are." It is my sincere advice. He continued, "Be a soldier. Everyone has to fight to survive in this harsh world. And you have also to fight to finish; accomplish the cherished dreams in right earnest."

The project for his rehabilitation was implemented on a broader canvas with the support of many. It was styled as 'Jeevan-Saathi'. Its advertorial proclaimed to arrange free service for the poor, economy package for the thrifty and custom design luxury for the rich. And Yogi Akshyayanand's frequent visit offered trust and confidence to the customers. After a marriage season, the people in the area were in praise of the services for 'Jeevan Saathi' and its social service. Akash has started living independently in the backyard of the office.

In the mean time Akshyay personally met his mother to persuade her to come back to them. He went and brought her to fulfill his promise. It was a real union of two grieving souls. She was too excited to see his son earning his living. To mark a new beginning, she took charge of the kitchen and asked Akshyay to leave only after meal. All three ate to each one's satisfaction and took rest a while. As sun declined, both parted to their place of duty.

It was about 4 pm. A police vehicle stopped before Akash's office and DCP got down along with another policeman. Akash was in panic instantly. He called his assistant to take care of them and went inside. Afraid of facing the reality, he called his friend Akshyay and informed him of the situation. He too was surprised and promised to reach immediately. Moments appeared days for Akash and he fidgeted. He asked one of the men employed to serve tea and request to wait a few minutes.

Akshyay arrived and saw DCP sitting on the sofa alone with a tea tray in front of him, untouched. "Good afternoon, sir. Why did you take the trouble of coming here? You could have sent for Akash." He stated not knowing where to begin.

"Oh, no. It's my work and I have to take the trouble. Isn't it?" he paused and continued, "But where is your friend Akash? And how are you here at this time?"

"Would you like to tell me about your visit?" Akshyay asked.

"It concerns him. I learnt a lot of praise about his work. I want to test." He replied.

Akshyay went inside. He found his friend totally shaken. He was in tears. Wiping his face, he spoke, "I have realized I was wrong. Since I started on the path you have shown, I felt like throwing million bricks out of my heart. I want to continue sincerely. The troubled past still appears before me like snippets from a movie scene and weakens me. Now the police have come and would not spare me."

His mother consoled, "Sometimes God takes a test. Don't worry. Your friend is here to take care of them."

And Akshyay encouraged him to face any situation that may arise. Both came to the office and Akshyay prepared tea for the DCP.

While taking tea, the DCP said, "I want you to handle the marriage of my daughter, scheduled next month. Please reserve a day for and let's finalize the arrangement including the charges."

Akash gained his lost confidence and the discussion followed. Akshyay marked with great appreciation the way he handled an important client. He was happy to note his transformation. Happy because his friend has discovered his latent talent inspired by a solemn purpose. His consciousness has expanded and good faculties have become alive. He went inside and explained his mother, "Maa, Akash is a professional businessman now. I am proud of him and I am sure, you will also be proud of him."

His mother blessed him saying, "I proud to have a son like you. You are a true friend indeed!"

Strive to do your duty and you will soon discover of what stuff you are made.

—Goethe

11

Thank You, God!

Only by knowing Him, can one pass beyond death.
There is no other path to the goal.

—*Shavatatara Upanishad*

"Chennai!!!" I screamed. "You can't do this to me. What blunder did I commit? Why am I being transferred?" my vociferous protest was spontaneous, my tone truculent and paroxysm at peak. But Kanupriya, the deputy director of HR remained phlegmatic. "It's not in my hands," she replied unruffled, as only the HR people can.

"You join coming Monday," she added. "and here are the tickets." Away from the bustle of Mumbai, I reached India's southern metropolis. "Culture shock" seemed too mild a term. The less said about the auto-rickshaw drivers the better. And the schedule followed by the denizens continues to baffle me. The city would wake up to life and activity at 4 am, and shut to slumber by 6.30 pm. Try explaining this to a Mumbaikar. I never understood nor would ever will. Finding an accommodation proved to be an onerous task. Once, a sub-broker rang up to say that a flat was available. "Let's meet the landlord at 6 pm, after office." I said. "Not possible, Madam." he replied. "Why not? Any problem?" I asked.

"After 6 pm is too late, Madam." And I had no answer. I gave up. A friend Divya was staying in the city, alone. I landed up in her flat after the first week of company-provided hotel accommodation was over. "If you want me out, you'll have to find me a flat," I said.

She has not bothered. Nor have I. We have been staying together for the past eight months, in the southern part of the city called "Thiruvanmiyur". The location has been rechristened "3-1-mayur" by Divya's family in their snail mails. The postal department seems not to mind. And Divya has not felt the need to correct them.

As time passed, I tried to get inured to the life in the city. One evening, Divya asked, "Keep the next Saturday free. We are invited to an informal gathering of some friends, by and large non-locals and I'll introduce you to some of them." Divya introduced me to Atul, or to put it more aptly he forced an introduction. It was his foible, perhaps of youth or my alert presence.

"I have never seen anyone except perhaps Sergei Bubka jump as high as him. "Dogs," he mumbled as he landed on earth again." Divya looked at him despairingly and continued,"When will your 'mortal fear' of the canine species end?"

I noticed Atul the dark, curly haired, moustached guy instantly a bit embarrassed but chatty through out.

The next weekend, I was in the market to get some necessities and I came across Atul.

"Is Divya home?" he enquired. I replied in the negative. "Are you afraid of dogs?" What was that? A pick-up line? I wondered. A pretty innovative one, I said to myself. I replied in the negative again. "Then will you come to the beach with me?" he asked. "And how is a visit to the beach related to fear of dogs?" I asked bewildered.

"If you have time, I will tell you the story of my encounter with the canine species."

"Well, yes. I have all the time on earth."

Atul accompanied me to our flat and made himself cosy in the beanbag. The tale he narrated seemed too amazing to be untrue and impossible to forget.

"The Thiruvanmiyur beach is the most fabulous beach I have come across and I'd readily spend all my nights up there but for the 'Notorious Dog & Co'. No, Geetha, they are not members of some gang, but actual dogs." he went on. And as Divya says, they can sense my 'mortal fear' of the canine species. The scalawags crowd around me in the beach and I have to plan an escapade before I can even have a decent bath or walk.

"The last visit to the beach I had an encounter with 'Notorious Dog & Co' ", he said. I went there alone and I had a group of not-so-lovely members of the 'Notorious Dog & Co' approach me and display their fangs, which would have done toothpaste companies proud. I felt the chill run down my spine. I calculated and traced the various routes back home. And before the two gangsters

could know my plan, I made a dart in the direction that would reach me to the safety of my flat in the shortest possible time.

Most members of the gang give up after a few yards. But two of the 'Notorious Dog & Co' seemed more persistent than usual. And they could definitely run faster than I. Mid-way to the safe haven, my flat, I was totally out-of-breath. While I tried to stop, pause or shout the two fanged beasts growled at me. They seemed eager to make me repent for encroaching into their territory. I looked at them. They stared back stoically. I pleaded. My eyes begging for mercy (I am pretty expressive). And they stare back unmoved. "Sorry dudes", I pleaded, "I won't encroach your territory alone again." They don't understand. They pretend to be as ignorant as the Chennai auto-rickshaw drivers. And given my "kunjum-kunjum" (minuscule) knowledge of 'bow-bow', I was unsure what to do."

(EDITOR'S WARNING: The adventure is NOT suitable for children and persons incapable of running and jumping as athletes!)

I barked, 'Bow-bow'

The gangsters looked at me again. A bit shocked.

'Boouuuuuuuuu Bhowwwuuuu,' I repeated.

'BHOOOW BHOOOU' replied one.

'Bow, Boouuuuuuuuu Bhowwwuuuu' I did an encore.

The other dog howled, 'BHHHHHAUUUUUUUUUUUUUUUU.'

And it created a melody of their own.

"Thank God". I heaved a sigh of relief, loud enough to wake Kumbhakaran (of Ramayana fame). "I am

safe," I exclaimed and danced in joy in the middle of the street. Therefore, I logically conclude they would not bite. I trusted the guys who made proverbs and sayings.

"Bow bou.... Thank you. Thank you," I replied joyfully. The dogs looked at each other baffled. The dancing male, especially if the male happens to be yours truly, did not provide an enticing view. The gangsters looked at each other again, stared at me and concluded I am not worth their time. They retreat in search of a saner victim."I have kept my promise. I never go to the beach alone", concluded Atul.

As I walked along his travail, I appreciated his angst and abomination for the 'canine species' and agreed to accompany him to the beach. The days and weeks passed and to my surprise, I realised that I was spending more time with him. I found him a unique person with a perpetual smile on his face, unless of course there was a dog nearby. He had the ability to see things most miss. He would smile when he saw a butterfly, laugh with the soft touch of the breeze and leave no stone unturned for people around to be happy. His theme, "Life has a lot to offer." In the spirit of "there is a lot to know if one is open to learning and there is a lot to experience if one is open to unlearning", I ventured to learn and unlearn a lot as I travelled with him to the virgin beaches in East Coast Road, the national highway that connects Chennai to Kanya Kumari. "Travel", I complained "is the pain of journey. Why can't we reach the destination in zero time, and enjoy the destination?"

"Life is not a destination but a journey. Learn to enjoy the process rather than the conclusion." he intoned.

"Stretch your hands and feel the breeze", he ordered as he zoomed at over 80 km/hr in his bike. I stretched my hands. I felt the breeze. I saw the sunset. I found myself smile and laugh. And gradually I felt myself indoctrinated into his way of life. I felt I had mastered the way to enjoy life!

One evening, I left office at 8pm. It was drizzling. I walked for a few minutes expecting a shower, wanting to get wet and feel the rain. But like the last three instances, the Rain God refused to oblige. On a street corner, I got off the auto-rickshaw and decided to walk the rest of the way to my abode. Still no rain. Only a mild drizzle. Akimbo.

I looked up. And crib, "God. There is not even a drizzle." Instantly the clouds growled. It rained with lightening and thunders. Within a few minutes, I was fully drenched. People ran for shelter. The crowd cuddled together under handbags-turned-umbrellas. The road seemed empty, but for a crazy lady standing, hands outstretched in the rain. She kicked the water, jumped at every puddle and laughed like a hyena.

It used to take ten minutes to cover the stretch, five if one ran in the rain. And thirty minutes if danced along the distance. I preferred the last option. Fully drenched I reached home, grinning like a baboon. Divya's aunty with two kids was sitting on the sofa. The kids giggled. I thought they've never seen someone dripping like a leaking water hose. Aunty-ji, already convinced I was a crazy nut, gave Divya a I-was-right-about-her look. If more confirmation of my insanity was needed, she got it when after dropping my mobile phone, watch and other paraphernalia in the ledge I went to the roof. To get wet some more (as if that was possible).

It was a climactic experience and I was in my element. I reflected, "There are times I wish I were young. There are times I feel HE makes me feel I'm still a child." I looked up towards the benevolent sky, because it is so enormous, so vast and endless like Him, to say "Thank you, God !"

12

Reflections

The desire of the moth for the star,
Of the night for the morrow,
Devotion to something afar
From the sphere of our sorrow. — *Shelley*

The incandescent sun blinding white in the sky has risen to its noon day peak. All colours flat, washed out, stripped of the richness given by the slanting light of the morning. Madhavi oblivious of the soul stifling heat that scorched fields and forests miles around preferred to sit in the front veranda of her home, brows puckered in concentration voyaging through the strange seas of thought alone.

A train of reflections appeared. How pleasant the childhood was! A song filled with happiness triumphant. Though she was born in a family that inescapably attached to the land, destined to live and die in pre modern agrarian society scrabbling at the unyielding soil as their ancestors did centuries ago, she was fortunate to have enjoyed warmth of love and tender care to sit by and timely food to sit down to. The school days were the climax of the halcyon passage with overwhelming appreciation from teachers, peers and neighbours. The day high school result was declared the whole village was ecstatic. It was a climactic moment and she was in her element. She secured third rank in the state board as a reward for her dedication and diligence. Filled with eager hope she thought that it was perhaps a new beginning – a door to new life!

The euphoria has been too short lived in the harsh reality. The last date for submission of application for admission to the science college remained only few days and she was yet to get permission from the parents. She is now torn between aspiration, yearning for higher studies and conservativeness, financial constraints projected by the family. It has been difficult even to imagine the course of action that may follow.

The longer she sat the more it reflected some powerful images from the past and it disturbed her. She always tried to nourish, by nature a positive attitude about life with enormous optimism. It has helped her transit through certain difficult moments over the past years. But this after noon, the very first time in her life her optimism has fled. She felt empty, extremely depressed, an emotion unknown to her till recently. It has been too hard to deal with. She was chilled to the bone.

She sat listless wondering about the finiteness of her existence finding no one to share her anxieties. She sighed in anguish, baffled. Suddenly the story of the mysterious *Yaksha* that has an abode in the trees surrounding the desolate pond at the far end of the village reflected to her.

"If the yaksha happens to see any ones reflection in that pond, the person would vanish instantly." Grandma has said on many occasions.

And she reasoned, "I can expect a reprieve from the impasse only if I visit the pond and subject my reflection in the pond to the *Yaksha*. Nobody will be able to trace me."

But before she could think about and plan for action, grandma's call interrupted,

"Madhu, where are you so long? What are you doing at this hot hour? I think even the stray dogs must have taken shelter in a cool place by now."

Madhavi was well aware of her affection and sympathies. She also knew that it was difficult for the grandmother to appreciate her ambition for college education as she lived in the grim boundaries of her penurious life with total devotion for rearing up the family. She did not learn reading and writing let alone higher education. The same was the situation with her innocent mother.

Another call from grandma made her apprehensive of volley of questions from parents if they got up and she immediately repaired to the room.

"Please don't worry about me. I am here with you. Now take rest." she hushed in a chortle.

She also lied down on the mat spread along side. But tossed and turned a while mind filled with uncertainty and foreboding. Then she walked about in the room for quite some time thinking. Had the parents openly told that they did not like her to attend college in a town alone she could have assured of her capabilities and determination to stand the test of time to uphold the dignity and honour of the family and parents. But she had no scope to resolve the financial aspects. As she lied down again fatigue overcame anxieties and drifted her to sleep.

She resolved,

"I have no alternative but to subject my reflection to the *Yaksha*. This would be a safe end."

She looked stealthily to confirm that grandma was in deep sleep. She also checked up that the parents were in side with the door of the room ajar. She walked out of the house with full knowledge that it was a dangerous mission and wished to leave no sign, no evidence of her passage. The distance of the pond, though about a mile appeared too distant in the blistering sun and still atmosphere. The familiar neighbourhood seemed too uncanny.

She hesitantly entered the area hedged with thorny bush and tropical trees. The deep blue water mass in the middle appeared like ice. The coolness and serenity of the place was a respite from the scorching heat. The sepulchral stillness that hung around scared her. But she reminded her of the resolve. She located a piece of broken rock that laid beside the water and seated herself. The reflection of her cameo face, diminutive features was clear as the water was without any ripple. The glare of the sun assaulted her but the fear that image might be blocked prevented her from shielding the face. She waited for some time and changed her position to another seat where the reflection could be seen from another direction. She repeated the process from different location not knowing exactly the abode of the Yaksha.

She waited and waited but there came no doling of the dove, no coo from the yonder trees. The waiting was proving interminable for her. She became restless and unable to account for it. She imagined only to be regretting for the wrong doing perhaps that there would be no scope to repair it. It seemed as if her eyes pierced through the storms of time to the terrors of eternity. She dwelt in private admonition on the future of the impenitent She felt totally drained, deprecated.

When the reflections were about to be concluded she sighed in anguish and looked up to find that the thunders rolled in. At the rumble of it, she glanced skywards, clouds spread in from the west, dark and thick. The brilliant sun light fell in to that false twilight that precedes a storm. The rumble became a roar that had her leaping to her feet and she started to dash away to safety, to shelter. And a bolt of lightening sizzling blue at the edges lanced in to the ground at her feet.

She woke up with a start, wet with perspiration blood pounding in her ears and her own gasp echoing. She heard her mother saying,

"Madhu, wake up. Your head master has come. He is talking with your father and wants to see you."

She found herself too untidy for meeting with the person whom she revered most as a guide and philosopher.

"How can I inform him that I am yet to get permission from my parents to submit the application?" she thought while washing her face and tending the hair.

Undecided, she went, paid her obeisance and stood beside in trepidation.

"How are you? What have you been doing during the holidays?" the head master asked. He continued after a brief pause, "I have come with good news for you. Government has notified that all the 'best ten students' from the board will be awarded merit scholarship to pursue higher studies up to post graduate level. Be happy and kick start the journey ahead."

"I will do my best, sir." she humbly assured.

The head master left after some refreshment and gradually the evening stars shone on the horizon. For Madhavi, it was indeed a moment of exhilaration. The tension that escalated to the peak has vanished. As night advanced, the moon quietly rose through the tranquil sky and a sleepy silence fell up on the village. Every one occupied their usual place for the night's rest, but she was too excited to sleep. She spent some time neatly filling in the application blank that remained unattended to, checking and re-checking for submission the next morning and thinking how to paint the future with renewed optimism.

The cock's crow signalled the dawn and alerted her that the night has passed by in moments. As she came out to welcome the bright morn she reflected "He is everything that exists under the sun – the lightening that destroys a home and the hand that builds it."

13

Cassandra

The body is not yours, the mind is not your mind..
The thoughts are not your thoughts; the self is only a concept.
Let's be delighted to be happy and alive with the flow of life!
—Upanishad

A March afternoon in the village, Swarnchampa. The unblemished sky after a quick shower, the mild fragrant breeze, the gleaming new leaves of the foliage, the sheen of the slanting rays of the declining sun were idyllic. The premises of Sat Gopal Agnihotri however were quiet and sombre with the exception of Radha's voice that resounded. She sat on the veranda of her tiny cottage, her bare back exposed to the sun and cautiously admonished while tending her daughter, Anusuya (Anu)'s hair,

"Look, you are now seventeen. And already attained puberty. You are no longer a child. You ought to be careful. Stop wandering with those lads. With His grace and Saab's blessings you are fortunate enough to read two years in college. What more for people like us? Now learn to take care of the household." She continued her instructions, "Keep the comb and oil in

continued her instructions, "Keep the comb and oil in proper place. Sweep the floor and arrange things. Don't pander over the bizarre thoughts for Heavens sake!" While Anu listened and affirmed in trepidation, she hurried saying, "I think Doctor babu has arrived."

Though inured to mother's constant jibbing, tears of frustration threatened to break free as she wondered for umpteenth time, "Why all these thoughts came to me?"

Radha met Dr. Sarat Chandra Das at the entrance and paid her obeisance, "Namaste Doctor babu. It is nice of you to have come so soon. Saab is restless since yesterday and we don't know what to do! I only sent for you."

"We just arrived and he is my son Ashutosh (Ashu). We have seen your Saab. Don't worry. He'll be alright, soon."

"I have already cleaned the room you normally occupy. Please get fresh while I arrange tea for you."

Though he knew her for quite some time, his imagination obdurately refused to encompass her continued devotion and service for Sat Gopal when all other including the near and dear ones have left. He thought it was one more manifestation of the variety and peculiarity of relationship of which he was a fascinated observer. He remembered the days when the place used to bustle with people around, servants, cooks, gardeners, drivers, errand boys, visitors and members of the local community seeking help, flattering for closeness of 'Saab' the sobriquet of Sat Gopal, the zamindar of Swarnchampa whose power, pride, preference, pastime spread miles around. The effortless warmth, amiable smile of Mr. and Mrs. Sat Gopal while welcoming an unknown guest touched his heart. He was fond of country and profession and from these tastes has arisen his principal source of enjoyment. And the locale full of pleasance in a sunlit swathe of soporific beauty with birds singing from tall palms to tamarind, neem to peepul and breeze playing in the clumps of the flowering bushes ideally suited his choice.

Gradually a symbiotic relationship developed as he yearned for a sojourn and Sat Gopal availed of his expert advice on health problems of the family. But he regretted that the place of pleasure has virtually turned to a portrait of gloom.

They entered the ornate living room, the interior almost comically crowded with chairs and tables, vases on stands, paintings on easels and every where in every vista, the arching, drooping, leaves of potted plants with its own historic light and odour and found Radha arranging tea and snacks for them.

"Sir, I am cleaning the room beside yours." she said and started to leave.

"It won't be necessary. I shall have to leave after the diagnosis because of commitments. Ashu is also a doctor and he'll continue to stay as long as required."

"Sir, if you permit I wanted to talk to you regarding my daughter." she tried to broach in.

"Is she unwell?"

"You would perhaps remember, I talked to you last time about her suffering because she sometime develops peculiar feeling in case any catastrophe is about to happen, which is unbelievable."

"Yes, I remember. I advised you to ignore those feelings and she should concentrate on her studies as she is a brilliant student. Sat Gopal has agreed to finance her studies. In case there is problem, I can also finance as long as she desires to study."

"But my predicament is that she has to get married soon, pray, before I die. Will this problem affect her at her in-law's place?" she expressed her angst.

"Ashu is an expert in this field. Let him discuss with her and we'll certainly find what need to be done." assured Dr. Das.

The doctors left after tea. The living room regained its sepulchral feel. As she started cleaning the table she felt a distant pang of loneliness and became schmaltzy. Like sunshine through the moving cloud memories came tearing back, pulling at her the way they always did. Her mind flashed back to the day she along with her husband arrived there in search of job and their meeting with Damayanti, Saab's wife. Her kindheartedness and caring nature entranced Radha couple. An intense emotional bond as twin sisters developed between them. Perhaps they shared similar values and attitude to life. She remained indebted for her love and compassion when she lost her husband in an accident. She tried to battle back tears remembering the parting moment of Damayanti and her promise to look after Saab.

What festered her was not only the memory of the good days and absence of ubiquitous Damayanti, but also Saab's failing state of health and above all Anu's prescience. She could only pray that it were not true.

Minutes later she reached Saab's room and waited. Dr. Das folded his stethoscope, put in his bag and quickly instructed his son who obediently affirmed.

"Please don't worry. You'll be fighting fit within a few days. In any case Ashu is here and I'll communicate with him regularly. And with your permission, I beg to leave lest it may be too late."

"I am grateful you could come. Have a nice journey. Hope we meet next when I am well." Sat Gopal intoned.

She came along with the doctors up to the car. Dr. Das left and Radha asked Ashu, "When you would like to have dinner, sir?"

"Please don't call me 'Sir'. Ashu is ok. And any time after 8 pm, please call me when dinner is ready," he replied and repaired to the room.

Radha admired his handsome features and affable manners. To her he mirrored sincerity and dignity. She called her daughter for help and busied for preparation of a diet and guest menu.

It was past eight in the evening when dinner was ready. She asked her daughter to take care of Saab, invited Ashu for dinner and served with motherly affection.

"Auntyji, thank you for the trouble you have taken. It is ages since I had such a delicious meal," he said. And while leaving informed, "I think it would not be inconvenient if I discuss with your daughter after breakfast, here."

"I'll tell her to be ready and meet you here. Pray you find some solution for her problem," she begged.

As scheduled, Anu came in smiling and greeted, "Good morning, Sir."

"Good morning, please sit," he said and looked at the refined beauty of the young woman's face that seemed to dissolve in to an expression of innocent wonder. Though she lacked ostentatious jewellery and garish attire, she seemed mystical and lovely. Her bucolic beauty displayed intense emotional appeal.

A few minutes passed with some introductory details and Ashu felt jiggy, his feeling of calm and normalcy completely evaporated. He was enthralled by her exquisite features, angelic manners and tone, sweet and soothing like honey. "Let's go out. It's pleasant outside," he suggested and she followed obediently. During the discussion that continued for about an hour, she answered honestly like a student in examination. "Well, that is all for the present. We'll continue afternoon," he said controlling his emotion. "Thank you, Sir," she said and left.

Ashu went inside his room and sat alone in quiet reflection, eyes closed. He wanted the thought let go, but she still stole her way into his mind. *'You can't always go by the first impression,'* he was telling himself. He spent the day brooding over except a few moments with Sat Gopal. During the dinner time Radha noticed his absentmindedness and ventured to ask, "I think the food is not to your taste. I should have checked up with you."

"Oh, no. it is very tasty. I was a bit preoccupied about Anu," he chuckled.

"Has she refused to answer your questions? I'll tell her. She has to cooperate and it is in her interest."

"No. She told all I wanted. I was thinking to talk to my father for some solution."

She felt relieved and left. But he could not sleep during the night. It seemed funny that the son of one of the reputed and wealthy medical specialist be so torn apart over a rural girl. *'Think positive! Expect the best and the best is what you'll get,'* he reflected and decided to talk to his father who has been his friend, philosopher and guide.

He thought of snatching a few moments of the quiet time, before he got totally involved with the problems of the patients and dialed, "Hellow."

"How are you Ashu? Hope all is well there."

"Bapa, I want to tell you the developments here; first, Sat Gopal uncle is improving fast. The infection is totally controlled and I think, he would be fit by tomorrow. Second, I talked to the girl, as you desired. She a wonderful young woman; quite sober, intelligent and haimish. She possesses of some power like Cassandra, the fabled character in Greek mythology endowed with the gift of prophecy but fated not to be believed. And her mother is not prepared to accept the immense magical potential she possesses, because that may upset their neat little universe. She feels profound sadness mingled with guilt and fear. And finally, during our interaction I felt a sense of adoration and ecstasy. It was as if paradise descended and I was living through the unforgettable moments in my life, entirely focused, the gentleness of the moving wind caressing me under the grace of the contemplating sky." He paused and continued, "I am baffled how I could be in love with an unknown girl. Please help me."

"Well, let me think it over. I would also like to discuss with Sat Gopal. He is very honest and pragmatic. But please keep it to yourself, till I reach there."

He felt a sense of unburdened ease and listened quietly to the voice of nature, understanding that invisible world always manifest itself in the visible world. He reflected, "Could she have ever imagined that one day I would be here to meet her?"

He spent the day mostly contemplating over the future with so innocent a woman who lived a penurious life and her compatibility with his social status. But he left the decision to his father and his wisdom. As per his advice, he maintained a distance with the girl, but in the emptiness around he felt he could touch her soul, hear the song she was singing while at work with absolutely nothing to distract her attention.

Next evening his father arrived and was surprised to find his son looking through the window into the darkness beyond.

"How are you dear?"

"Good Evening, Bapa. Have you been long?" he apologised.

"I just came. Any new development?"

"Well, yes. Uncle is fully cured and there is no need for us to stay here."

"Let me meet Sat Gopal," he said and left.

"Welcome back Doctor. I am fine except a little weakness. And I think, your son is a better doctor. Very matured even at this young age, I observed."

"I am proud and honoured for your compliment. I pray he excels in his profession."

He then narrated the details he learnt from his son and sought his valued opinion.

"I know them so long. I confirm that they are very sober, sincere, hard working and trust worthy. And Radha is chaste. In spite our repeated request to shift to this almost empty mansion, she still prefers to maintain the distance and takes care of every thing because of her promise to my wife in her deathbed. I may also tell you that I have willed what ever I have to Anu."

"Ashu is my only son. I want him happy in life. Please tell me whether they would make a good couple."

"I am sure she would prove to be a good life partner and I pray for their happy married life." Sat Gpoal felt exhilarated and requested Radha for arranging a feast in honour of the doctors.

After dinner, Dr. Das called Radha and politely proposed, "I hope you don't mind if I take Cassandra (Anu) as my daughter." And she looked in askance. Sat Gopal intervened to clarify, "We have discussed and decided that Dr. Ashutosh and our Anu would make a good couple. Your blessings are required."

Radha stood transfixed and ineffable. Blinking away tears she looked in acquiescence. She instantly floated, buoyed by the warmth generated by His grace and their thoughtful decision. Her reverie was broken when Sat Gopal asked her to pack Anu's clothes as they would leave next morning. He also informed that Anu would join a college of her choice and marriage would be only after she completed her studies.

The night was quiet except for the sound from the nocturnal insects. The mother and daughter retired in silence but were too excited to sleep. Radha never believed there would be time like this. While she contemplated shining dreams for the future of her daughter, chuckled, "Maa, I feel like a princes in a fairy tale!" Overwhelmed with happiness they could hardly guess when they drifted to sleep.

The morning sun was riding across the sky wrinkled with rippling gray clouds and up in the heights the breeze was mingling with clouds along gently. The air here in the plain seemed to jostle with nothing but the presence and names of 'Anu' and 'Ashu' with the knowledge of the laurels, aparajitas and azaleas. Dr. Das bade fare well and drove off with his son and Cassandra nestling close. Sat Gopal and Radha stood waving behind...

14

One Fine Afternoon

Talent develops itself in solitude and character in a life stream.
—Goethe

'Divine dictates every where, neither scholastic performance nor valour.' Thus goes the *Shruti*. Some are fortunate to have more than what they deserve while some struggle and achieve less. This is perhaps the law of life. My inexorable travail confirms the truth of the statement. Destiny scripted only struggle for me which I have accepted and I continue enjoying the challenge in my pursuit. As a votary of existence I believe life is always half full and not half empty. And in the spirit of Mark Twain's thought, 'sorrow can take care of itself, and a joy when shared gets manifold' I share some pleasant moments from my eidetic memory.

It was first week of July 1961. I was filled with excitement seeing a ray of hope in the horizon. I was to take admission in the Pre University Science class of the Fakir Mohan College, Balasore. I have received a card asking me to report at 9 AM next Monday along with my high school mark-sheet, transfer certificate and a character certificate from the head master of the school I studied.

In those days there was no direct bus from our village to Balasore and one had to walk about five kilometer for a public conveyance available at some intervals. I gleaned information and settled for the 3 pm bus a day earlier as optimal and convenient. I set my bare foot on the sandy soil with a small cotton bag containing some certificates and a pair of shorts and shirt. I walked alone on the narrow sandy path changing sides to avail of the shades of some trees as the blistering midday sun continue shining in the azure sky over head. The walk was fast and the thoughts were still faster.

I reached the bus stop sweat soaked. As no one was around, I thought either it was too late or too early. In any case I preferred to stand under a shadowy tree for respite. The place had a deserted look as heat and sweat forced people indoors. I eagerly waited for some one to talk to. Some time passed. A person came with two bundles loaded on his shoulder and asked me, "Has the bus to Balasore left?" Though I was expecting a reply to the same question, I calmly replied, "Let us wait." A few more people arrived and the lone tea stall was opened by the entrepreneur-cum-operator after his siesta. He announced that there was enough time for the bus as well for tea. I could not appreciate why people took hot cup of tea and sweat in the sultry weather.

The bus finally came to a grinding halt and people rushed for boarding. The conductor intervened allowing alighting first and the passenger to buy ticket before getting in. As I threaded in, I was drifted towards the front and managed to stand holding a bar behind a seat. The bus moved on. The soft wind that pierced its way across the wooded glade was respite for all of us. As I looked for a comfortable place to stand to prepare for more than an hour and a half to reach the destination, I overheard a discussion, more of a debate among three passengers seated together. They were well clad and appeared erudite from the effusion and eloquence of their speech. The topic being school, teachers and students interested me and I turned facing their side only a short distance away.

The debate as it emerged centred around the role of teachers and students in the examination result. While one member was vociferous that teachers have potential to mould pupils for success, the other was equally firm that intelligence and interest of the students are critical. The third remained by and large a moderator. With my background as a student of a rural high school with limitations in knowledge and experience, I felt both are equally important and complementary. And my interest grew to learn the fine line from their discussion.

The bus moved on passing through jungles, meadows, hamlets in its rhythm. Inside, some were dosing, some indifferent and various small groups engaged interacting on the failure of monsoon and implication there on. My focus was on the teacher-student debate and some excerpts of the arguments with exception to slight variation of the quintessence follow:

"I owe my success to my teacher." The one supporting the teacher's role put forward convincingly and persuasively.

"You probably are ignorant of your own potential for the success." The other advocating intelligence of the student quipped.

"It is my personal experience. And many of my friends also feel the same."

"All of you have seen this year's high school result. A boy from Kumara High School is among the best ten. And I know the school. There has not been any teacher worth the name for any subject. How could he score such high marks?" It was the other's telling argument.

The reference to my school was exciting and a direct reference to my performance in the board exhilarating. I could feel hairs on my body bristle with apprehension. *'To be an object of importance is some times a pleasure,'* I reflected. While I appreciated the positive things said about me for their true value, instantly I was in the horns of a dilemma; should I reveal my identity or remain incognito. As I have been absorbing their manners, their speech and their arrogance carrying along the incurable air of importance, I felt safe to opt for the later and share the appreciation as we always, as human beings, search for. I hoped there would perhaps be opportunity to meet on 'well fought fields'.

I never believed there would be time like this; the life's poetry brought to reality forcing forward, step by step towards the pulsating wave of happiness which has once been lost. I learned to appreciate His marvel that created roses amidst thorns. The life affirming joy was broken and I came to attention as people inside started rushing to get down. I heard the moderator mention, "I would certainly like to meet the wunderkind." I joined all to alight at the last stop and hurried towards destination.

The journey in the memorable afternoon has been a sunlit moment and a source of great pleasure. It continues to be an inspiration in 'the endless spiral of my ascent and fall' in life.

Life is not a matter of milestones but of moments.

— Rose F. Kennedy

15

Marriage in the Family

Life is not a brief candle. It is a splendid torch!

—George Barnard Shaw

It was mid April in Dharampur, a hamlet not far from the eastern coast. Summer has set in. The tender leaves of most of the tropical trees have gradually turned bright green. While the spring flowers are on the wane, a light aroma of the mango flowers still prevails in the serene atmosphere.

The residence of Gautam and Gourang brothers has been a hub for the last three days with the preparation of an ornate pandal for the guests, their seating and eating arrangements, arrival of guests, their ceremonial welcome, children's jabbering and mother's jibbing, group discussions and advising, and in addition the super imposing firing of the rollicking remixes and foot-thumping bollywood hits from a hi-fi system.

Yesterday was the day of marriage, one of the days packed with ceremonial functions. The day started with rituals amidst the *sehanai* and drums beats and ended with the marriage procession that left the premises by about 10.30 PM led by a music troupe, 'melody' along with family members, relatives, friends and neighbours, invited and uninvited. In spite of every effort to get them started by 9 PM, as promised it was late. Late because the rituals could only be completed by a specified number of women and most of them were busy hours applying makeup, doing hair till they were convinced that they were still attractive and men would ogle them and chat them up. The girls sequined and frivolous, eyes bright flaunted exotic feathers that winged out ardent effort to be recognized and loved. The men too followed with garish attire to look rich and famous and boys put on best dresses and shoes for dancing to the tune of the 'melody'.

The brides place being at walkable distance Gautam decided to reach alone directly instead of following the procession, after a cold water bath and bit of relaxation. He has been so engrossed with entertaining the guests that he has to be satisfied with some random bites instead of timely food he is attuned to.

Today, it has been full of activity since early hours of the morning when the newly-wed couple arrived. The welcome ceremony with the drum beats, blowing of conches and the *hulo-huli* of the woman folk not only energised their usual languid premises but also awakened the neighbourhood from their deep slumber during the most pleasant and peaceful dawn.

Gautam, Gaurang along with few close relatives who assumed responsibility for conducting and completing the marriage ceremony arrived walking and discussing their likes and dislikes which was inappropriate to talk to at the bride's place. While the mood was to continue, hunger drove Gautam to skip chit-chat. He felt the need to finish morning bath lest the ladies would take priority. He begged leave to complete his personal morning necessities. As he came chanting *shlokas* invoking His blessing the morning, birds were whistling in the wild lilacs and the mist that hung around in pre dawn was beginning to rise and die away. To his surprise he noticed those same ladies busied themselves applying makeup even before bath. He wondered, "Is it that they are examining their faces in compact mirrors to repair the damages caused by their dream lovers or to ensure looking as attractive as they met in dreams as while awake?"

He finished the usual morning rituals and looked out for some one to appreciate his problem, but found all too engrossed in eating, talking and fully involved with only the dearest ones. The feeling that 'no one cared for him now' devastated him and he reflected, "I have lived alone but never felt so lonely, uncared for, deliberate or inadvertent. Travail and tribulation notwithstanding, I have consciously lived with unconditional love for the family and the relationship which proved to be steadfast seemed collapsing."

Hungry, fidgety and concerned, he paced back and forth in a small vacant room and tried to shut his eyes resolutely on the bleak impersonal room and willed himself to sleep with stomach filled with fresh water from the well, but sleep too eluded. As he lied down eyes closed, memories kept flashing into his mind like the scenes from a popular picture. The scenes remained the same: it was the marriage of his brother about four decade ago and now his son's. The actors have changed; some are no more, others added more grey hairs and quite a few new. The change was perceptible. While a spirit of love, care, share and willing participation as a homogeneous group was in the air then, the present scene shadowed devouring everything on their path like fiery, merciless larva, totally unconcerned of the world around. It was too difficult for him to absorb. He needed someone to talk to, share his feelings. Uncontrolled tears rolled down his cheeks. He remembered how his parents were concerned with: before he entered home after bath, breakfast used to wait for him and his wife would panic if he was late a few minutes. And now they being no more, loneliness hounded him deep inside.

The experience of the life's reality impoverished his opinion: life seemed to rip out leaving him in darkness facing abyss, as though he has fallen into a black hole and was being torn apart by the forces he couldn't fight. His onetime menacing determination, remorseless patience seemed to collapse. Wild thought pummelled, "Is this the reward for my total devotion for nurturing relationship? How can my dear ones be so indifferent? Why this change? What could be the reason for such a change? And does this signal the future that would follow?" He went on thinking for some definite and plausible answer. Though logically he could conclude that the instant situation called for decisive action, he reflected, "As I have only loved them, I have never bothered to judge them. Immediate action would perhaps be inappropriate. It may also have irreparable consequence. More over, the reception is slated for tonight and my active participation is necessary."

Ignoring hunger, indignity he came out. While the aroma of the spring flowers continues to scent the environment, the iridescent eastern sky has changed with the morning sun ascending in the unblemished azure sky. The piercing bright rays dazzled him. He however couldn't miss the sight that unveiled with gratifying clarity the wicked widows, cruel cousins, kind aunts and lecherous grandmas who dropped by to see the bride's face and were returning passing judgments to initiate gossip on the bride's rating that varied from 'good', 'not so good' to 'does not match the family's respect'..sharing with in-house relatives who were busy munching mouthful sweets, *paan* or tea cup in their hands. As family for him has been a temple of peace, he conveyed the departing guests, "The real beauty lies only in virtues and values and not in the colour of the complexion. And let's..pray Him to usher in her the real beauty."

The visitors continued their gossip ignoring the remark. He too had duty to attend to, particularly the arrangement required for lunch and the evening function. As he moved by an elderly neighbour came in and praised him for his care for the family. He requested him, "Uncle, please do bless the bride and have tea before leaving."

"Son, I am here since long and have been observing things happening, people around including you. And I am sure, you have not yet taken anything and you are offering me. What a strange world!"

Fighting back tears, he replied, "We have to take care of the guests. It's our responsibility."

"Well said. Pray, people realize their duty to some extent. In any case we'll meet in the evening." mentioning in passing he left. He sat down pensive for some time and decided to chase the wild thoughts away with a simple resolution that dictated commitment, "Well, I think, I have the strength to accept whatever God grants. And I have to live in the present that calls for action." He contemplated, "Though our human condition makes us tend to share only the best of ourselves, because we are always searching for love and approval, it is not always possible that we win."

Oblivious of the rising heat and hunger he devoted energy in organizing the function. By the time sun set in the horizon, the guests started to pour in. He thought he was in for trouble, but they surprisingly limited their interest only to eating and it was well taken care of. The reception in the evening was to the satisfaction of all. The in-house guests repaired for a well deserved rest. And he, left to himself surmised from his memory, the life's philosophy: "Don't expect to get anything back, don't expect recognition for your effort, don't expect your genius to be discovered or you have to be understood. Complete the circle not out of pride, inability or arrogance, but simply because the existing things no longer fit in your life. Choose the door, change the record, clean the house and get rid of the dust. Stop being who you were, become who you are!" It's perhaps the only way to fight back negativity, to cherish beauty, relationship, triumphs, love and laughter.

Blessed is he who expects nothing, for he shall never be disappointed.
—Benjamin Franklin

16

A Dream Accomplished

True happiness is that Reality we touch when all is lost.

—E Raymond Rock

"It has been an unusually quiet day, today." Adarsh felt while taking lunch, alone in his spacious house he has acquired and occupied for about six months now. Though the part-time maid has taken permission for leave of absence, no visitors and not even a telephone since morning. The initial period of his stay here passed getting settled, meeting a few friends whom he knew earlier, acquaintance with the neighbours, purchases and locating sources for the necessities. No sooner people learnt about his academic interest and that he had a wide ranging experience, young aspiring students and anxious parents have been visiting for free consultancy. He, in his own interest welcomed them and discussed with them their predicaments suggesting alternatives.

He started thinking, "Have I taken the right decision to live here, all alone?" But it was his sovereign decision, partly driven by his desire to get personal space and in part, not to interfere with the routine of the parental home. He has also discussed with his son and daughters. It was hard to convince his younger brother.

His parental home is about 25 kilometer from this town in a rural setting. Though it is spacious enough to accommodate him including his paraphernalia, he always felt the absence of his parents and wife. Sometimes he even did not approve of the way the affairs are managed. Once he surmised, "Perhaps, I have become fastidious and they continue to be abstemious."

It is but natural to have developed a different perspective of life as he has a wider vision: extensively traveled in India and abroad, well read on a vast range of authors and subjects contrary to his brother having limited exposure to life and activity in the village. Reading and writing has fascinated him and from this taste has arisen his principal enjoyment.

He wanted to rest a while to put all roving thoughts at rest, but painful recollections intruded which he could not repel. He felt the need for someone near and dear with whom to share his anxieties. The pleasant weather, soft breeze could not bring cheers to his mood. As he tried to close his eyes, memories, sweet and sour flashed like Bollywood mega-starrer on cinemascope: memories of idyllic childhood amidst all pervading scarcity, but soaked in love of grand-parents, parents and doting sisters including neighbours; memories of carefree student days in school and colleges, despite burdened apprehension to maintain the academic excellence and the turbulent professional career with many highs and lows and last but not the least the untimely demise of wife.

By nature he has been able to maintain composure in difficult circumstances, and in particular when he used to read or write. He displayed supreme concentration warmed by the fire of imagination, oblivious of the environment around. It was different that afternoon.

He moved to the terrace to the cozy corner and sat down comfortably with books and paper on the table. These were his companion in pleasure and pain, hope and despair. While inside he swathed in troubled past, outside external disturbances distracted. The unblemished blue sky, patches of drifting clouds that used to keep him absorbed with its vastness and magnificence for long hours could not attract him. He applied deep breathing technique to quiet passing thought and closed eyes. He listened to the birds, street hawkers, children giggling and adult cacophony. He imagined how wonderful the home with pulsating life of a joyful family would be. And instantly a distant cry of a baby pictured a sombre scene in a wanting home where either the mother has been too occupied with domestic trivia or uncaring to the baby's needs. The diversity of enriching experience enlivened his senses for deep contemplation.

His focus shifted to an analysis of his life in retrospect: 'what I have gained and what I have lost?'; fully aware of the fact that nature always combines opposites like day and night, waxing and waning moon. Gain or loss had to have their share in life's balance sheet. Seated alone in quiet reflection, senses alive with anticipation he remembered a passage from Guruji Rabindra Nath Tagore,

"All my life I believed that I have the strength to accept what ever God grants. Till date my faith has never been put to tests. But now I believe the time has come. To test the strength of my belief, I have visualized many kinds of misery-poverty, humiliation and even death of dear ones. Still I did not lose faith in Him. Deep down within me, there is pain. I go about my usual duties, but the hurt lingers. Even when I sleep, the pain gnaws at my rib from where has it come to cast a dark shadow on my full moon. The lie of the past sorrows which masquerades as joy tears me apart."

It resembled his present status. His subconscious being a repository of facts associated with life, snippets of events that have left indelible impression on the black slate of his mind and that factored as assets and liabilities appeared on a broad canvas:

The childhood has been an idyllic passage that continues to elate me. It has been a great source of solace in my travail: what ever be the weather, the period continues to remain sunlit to brighten and heighten my spirit. I catapult my vision to glimpse the unique opportunity as the only child in an extended family enjoying everybody's attention: parents, neighbours, cousins. Mother's caring nature, father's attachment to hold close even after a day's tiring hard work are unforgettable, indeed.

My enrollment in the village primary school was a story in itself. New experience to mix with friends, work and learn new things under loving teachers was absorbing. I happened to be good at studies and my excellence became example for others to follow. It was sort-lived. As the village had only primary school, education in high school required finance for boarding, which was beyond the scope for my penurious family. A commitment for a four year programme was beyond comprehension. Despite securing a scholarship, my life seemed to hit a dead end. With shattered dreams, I used to curse myself for ill fate and weep alone with no way to look forward. And finally, I accepted to be a peasant, as my parents and grand parents had been.

Time changes everything and such a change came in my life. A new school opened in the neighbouring district and I was offered a freeship. I took admission after a year's discontinuance. By His Grace I passed out high school in flying colours securing a rank in the state board. The school and village rejoiced on the occasion, but I was torn deep inside with the reality that it was end of my academic career. Yet again, development turned to favour. Pandit Jawaharlal Nehru, the visionary prime minister announced a scheme awarding national scholarship for meritorious students. I greeted the news with great relief- I was one of the recipient. My hope soared to empyrean heights. The scholarship structure was sixty rupees for general studies and one hundred and ten per month for pursuing technical education. It heightened hope for accomplishing a cherished dream.

An analysis in retrospect would certainly evince that had I continued study without a break for a year, perhaps high school would have been the end of the career. It would be rather difficult to conclude whether it was a random coincidence or His design. In any case, I was fortunate to avail of the benefit. It helped me to graduate from one of the most reputed institute with a professional degree.

The care free student life too ended. Laden with responsibilities, though there was no imposition I decided to take up a job. There were limited choices. To continue with the academic line, perceived to be my forte, I accepted an offer to join as lecturer in the institute I studied with scope to simultaneously pursue post graduate programme. I thought it was a blessing in disguise to continue studies and earn. As luck would have it, circumstances did not favour. With change in the management structure, the job offer was withdrawn and we were asked to continue with studies only. Most in the similar situation left in search of other avenues. I too shifted to an institute in my state as a faculty.

Little did I know that in real life, academic excellence and competence were not enough to be successful. Even in my own state, I was treated with vengeance as to an outsider who had invaded their territory. I felt strangulated. In the mean time, I received offer of selection to join Government of India in the cadre of Engineering Services in Grade I. All those whom I respected and trusted, without exception advised me to accept the offer. And I joined.

My first impression, I choose to be in fire from the frying pan. Far from near and dear ones, not even a single soul with whom I was acquainted with it was a nightmare. The office filled with files and life full of grandeur due to pomp of power rather than lights of thought haunted me. And there was no escape. I completed a respected management degree, but it also could not help me shift. I got mired to the compulsions and adapted. Academic was my flare which I lost for good.

While I dared for reason to prevail, there were times when inconsistencies of official life, forced by circumstances of bureaucratic authority I had to put my intellect to rest. Perhaps it was pragmatism. Though the decisions were instant, some times I wondered whether it was right.

The desert too has an oasis. Amidst turbulence and travail of the life's journey, I had an opportunity to extensively travel in India and abroad, interacted with eminent persons of different walks of life at national and international level. The family enjoyed a stay abroad; children studied and had a glimpse of other social and cultural environment that broadened their horizon.

The period of active engagement too ended and a new phase of life began. To some, it would mean care free and leisure while others might as well feel isolated and passive. I had some plans to engage myself and at the same time pursue certain interest which I cherished long. His wishes however were different. I was constrained to remain at Delhi for a long period, where I was not at home and by the force of sheer circumstances my attention diverted to a different stream. Had I been a loser, again?

The question disturbed him. A balance sheet for a life's accomplishment and disappointment are not so easy, particularly when one finds himself as a shipwreck sailor alone in a desolate island. But Adarsh's erudition and philosophical bent of mind helped him to attune his attitude inspired by the thoughts of Voltaire to Radhakrishnan. Voltaire believed, "Every player must accept the card life deals him. But once they are in hand, he alone must decide how to play in order to win the game." And Radhakrishnan echoed similar thought,

"Life is like a game of bridge. We did not invent the game or design the cards. We did not frame the rules and we cannot control the dealings...to that extent, determinism rules. But we can play it well or play it badly. A skillful player may have poor hand and yet win the game. A bad player may have a good hand and yet make a mess of it. By exercising our choice properly, we can control steadily all the elements and perhaps eliminate all together the determinism of nature."

With these rationale, he was about to quiet the mind practicing what he learnt from the teachings of mystics and seers, the sound of the call bell broke his reverie. Unaware of the real position, who and how long has someone been kept waiting, he jumpstarted to open the door. To his surprise, he found an unexpected visitor. Mr. Choudhury, his next neighbour was standing alone; mood askance. Before he could extend an apology for keeping him waiting, Mr. Choudhury said with supplication,

"Hope, I have not disturbed you."

"No, not at all. Please come in and be comfortable. I'll join you in a minute." He replied and went inside for washing his face.

"Would you like coffee or tea?" he asked.

"No formality please. I don't want to trouble you."

"Everyone comes up with the same excuse, because I live here alone. In any case, it is tea time and we shall chit-chat over a cup of hot brew. What is your choice?"

"What ever is your regular routine."

In a few minutes he came with tea and biscuit in a tray and Mr. Choudhury could not believe how it could be so soon. He compared his home; he would have to wait for at least half an hour for the same and it was less than even ten minutes. He thanked for the tea and his immaculately neat house.

"How do you maintain it?" he asked again after some time.

"Well, living alone is a different story."

"I learnt your son is very well placed in US and your daughters are alsc well educated and in job."

"I want personal space for myself and at the same time, they should have freedom to choose the way they want to live."

"Nice thought, but don't you feel being alone? I don't even see a TV. How do you spend time?"

"I have a TV, which I use sparingly. And there are ways to spend time usefully. It depends on one's interest and habit."

The pleasantries continued for some time and both finished the tea. Considering that weather outside was pleasant, both moved up to the terrace.

The overarching sky, soft fragrant breeze, a crane flying by with its moon-white wings gleaming and the knocking of the wood pecker in search of water created an ambiance that would enthral any nature lover. And they started strolling leisurely. Though Adarsh was anxious to learn the purpose of his visit, he thought it impolite to ask and remained quiet. He drew two chairs and offered a seat. In the course of interaction, he could realize that Mr. Choudhury was not happy as he would like to be at present for various reasons. He seemed disturbed about his life after retirement, not so good performance of the children and suchlike. He thought of sketching a range of insights into human nature gleaned from reflections. He said, "Life does not generally offer what we desire. We are generally worried about the future, which is beyond our control and hold inquest on the past that cannot be altered. In the process we ignore the present which truly exists. We have to accept life as it is and assign importance and meaning to each moment. I too have spend sometime evaluating gains and losses. This is because we are programmed to believe on the external manifestation and search for happiness outside. Our thoughts and actions are oriented to the external world. The myth governs our life." He continued, "But nature teaches us to be in harmony with the stream of events, with the stream of life full of love and compassion, surrendering to the ever flowing stream and belonging to the unity."

He quoted Osho saying, "Develop just courage to be silent and alone. Slowly, slowly you start feeling a new quality of yourself, a new aliveness, a new beauty, a new intelligence which are not borrowed and are growing within. It has roots in our existence."

All it needs is to overcome the inertia. Just as a potter's wheel set in motion turns for a long time, the wheel of thinking, the wheel of discrimination would revolve and stir the soul to take the right path. And he concluded that 'it is prudent to be happy with what we have rather than aspiring for what we don't'.

Mr. Choudhury sat apoplectic. And finally he said, "You are right. I think you have solved my dilemma to a large extent. Please do drop by. Mrs. Choudhury would be happy to meet you."

By the time he bade good bye, the sun was setting in the western horizon, melting the blue sky to orange and red. He thought, "It has been worrying me that I have pain in my finger, but when I see that others are living without feet, I realize what the reality is. The reflections from the world around convinced me that it is no wisdom to worry that the glass is half empty, it is worth enjoying that it is half full that suffices my need." It echoed the teachings of Osho, "Life is an opportunity to create a meaning. It is a poem to be composed, it is a song to be sung and a dance to be danced."

And he intoned, "Considering my economic background from birth to date, I have moved up the ladder notwithstanding the sporadic downs and it is a happy note that my dreams accomplished!"

There is only one success : to spend your life in your own way.
—Christopher Morley

17

Groom Search

Most of us tend to embroider our memories to suit the picture of ourselves that we would like the world to see.

—Andrew Crofts in 'Ghostwriting'

I intend to tell you a story; more appropriately unfold a drama that happened in real life. And before I venture, I think it would be appropriate to acquaint you with the background: a prologue. I am Dhananjay Dandapat. Well, such a name has been assigned to me by my grand parents, who spent their life in penury and perhaps overenthu-siastically took a prognostic view to get richness through a suitable name and of course their blessings. My parents being *karmayogins* hardly had time to get involved or interfere in the mundane ceremony of naming their son. To them, 'all that happens is His will and we all should honour it'. Looking in retrospect, I think the values have overwhelming influence on me and I continue to live with them in grace.

My family: I boast to have fathered two daughters and a son. I had a decent job and offered my children sufficient freedom as well as support to pursue a career of their choice. In the spirit of the axiom that is relevant to those in the educated middleclass that, 'there are only two lasting bequests we can give to our children - one is roots and the other wings'; I endeavoured to offer good education to the children for security and independence.

The elder daughter, on completion of her post graduation in literature got married and now well settled in life. That she is happy is a great source of pleasure for me, like any father. The other daughter and son are professionals from reputed institutes and are enjoying with nice placement and pay packet. And as a father, I feel it my duty and responsibility to get them married and see that they are happy. My wife, by nature being spend-fast, spent her life too fast, leaving me alone to face this harsh world.

And now with regard the caption for the story regarding finding a groom for my daughter, I do believe that 'selection' should be more appropriate than 'search' to offer equality; but with due apology and respect to the feminine sect, I thought it inappropriate to hurt the male predominance in our society by ignoring the same.

We know that marriage as an institution has undergone sea change since human appeared on earth. Today, it is accepted in society and sanctified by law that marriage is a biological, physical as well as emotional necessity; though a section believes, at least philosophically, that it is union of the two individual souls, pre ordained in heaven. The age, legally prescribed eighteen for the girls and twenty-one for boys not withstanding, it ranges from pre-birth betrothal to near death nuptial as all of us read periodically in press and also come across on other media channels.

Against this background, I intend to come to the story proper: to narrate my experience on the search for a suitable groom which is factual in content and unbiased in presentation, though embellished. It would certainly be representative sample relevant to a wide section.

We belong to a conservative society. Its social and cultural norms dictate, though there are no written rules, that a girl should be married by the age of twenty three- twenty four at the latest and a boy by twenty five to twenty six. Accordingly, a number of good proposals came through relatives, friends and well wishers when my daughter was at this age. I could not decide in favour of immediate marriage as it would have resulted in leaving the professional programme she has been pursuing in jeopardy. And I admit, there has been a bit delay due to circumstance beyond our control.

It was about two years back. She stepped into twenty eight and I felt alarmed. I discussed with the children and it was decided that not only the marriage proposals to be considered but vigorous effort need to be made in this direction. My son being a computer savvy professional, immediately offered to register in one of the popular sites for suitable response. It is indeed a huge canvas where anybody can place his/her details. To begin with no fee is charged; but in case contact details are required, either the bride or the groom has to pay for the same. Interacting through the internet was very interesting and enlivening.

A large number of probable would be posted on the e-mail address provided every day. I started taking printouts of every possible candidate for the first few days, and soon realized that to handle this information would require a secretariat. I set two critical factors for short listing; first, the boy should be well qualified and second, he should be placed in a city, though metros preferred. The criteria were well thought of to provide for an opportunity for the bride and groom whether to take up any assignment, in the event of a decision. Keeping in view the parameters and my personal judgment regarding compatible age and caste, the big list was screened and print out taken for the preferred ones.

The next step was to seek the consent of the groom, which was quite easy with the clicking of the mouse. Then starts the waiting time because it involves taking a decision based on the available information by the candidate, friend or relation who may be responsible. Those who offer acceptance, technically comes in the zone of further negotiation. As I have explained earlier, either side has to pay the promoter of the site to get contact details. The process begins with asking for detailed CV, horoscope, photo and family details. After a few such instances, I prepared a set of standard information and sent immediately. While sending the details, I used to ask politely for similar information about the candidate and family, which I thought a genuine requirement.

My experience in this regard is varied, too. While very few come forward with the information, many feel it derogatory to their male chauvinism and respond in a manner to show their insinuation.

The process in so far as it involved the internet has been exciting: on-line information on an unimaginable range of candidates on a platform to choose from, almost all basic information provided and the intent for acceptance or denial. A technological marvel, indeed. But when it comes to human behaviour, my experience has been that by and large the mindset remained primitive. The genuineness of the information content however are not assured. In one case we realized, the candidate has placed his details in three different names with different age and academic qualification. Perchance during interaction, the daughter-in-law of the family mentioned the true age and qualification without realizing the implication. The people no doubt have developed new age computer knowledge, but they are yet to be honest with themselves, I thought. The actual human behaviour is perhaps largely conditioned by the culture that embodies value sets.

One of my experiences would certainly reflect the mindset and approach to life. On receiving information about a candidate who is professional and in the process of starting a business, I went to invite him so that both the bride and the groom get an opportunity to meet, though for a few minutes. My objective was to rule out at least their incompatibility and adverse reaction, if any. I also wanted to get a feel of the person, his attitude, his capability and his aspirations.

To initiate the discussion, I elaborated a bit about our family: that we owe lineage to a rural agricultural setup and my parents are no more. My brother takes care of the farming of the agricultural land we have. His children, like mine are employed outside. I earnestly expécted some information about his family background. But to my surprise, he asked,

"How do you get your share?"

"Now a day's agriculture is not so profitable and I have never thought of a share to date."

"But you must get your share. It's legitimate."

"On the contrary, I try to help when ever he has any finance requirement." I mentioned to divert.

And to my query regarding his family, the only information that he would certainly have a big setup in Delhi in future was forthcoming. I felt, though I was constrained to express, that the boy was too ambitious. His overt interest and emphasis on pecuniary matter reminded me of father Pat Conner, who with his 40 years of experience in marriage counseling noted that 'most marriage that founder do so because of money- she is thrifty, he is on his 10th credit card'. I returned with bruised feelings.

I presume, an account of my experience with each individual groom may not only be burdensome, but also boring and thus I present a differentiated group spectrum. I may inform that some more response have came from the matrimonial ad in all Indian metro cities through a leading national daily including a local newspaper of my state and these have been added to the statistical universe. To my surprise, a wide range of uniquely different experience emerged.

Of the two dozen candidates in the scope for negotiation, about half a dozen resulted in height mis-match: grooms too tall in comparison to the bride.

A set of candidates who work in metros and live alone expressed initial enthusiasm perhaps due to the likely financial advantage that would accrue and eventually help towards a better standard of living. I too was excited, as it matched my specification. While initial acceptance was smooth and fast, information relating to their parents or elders who would be responsible to talk to for proceeding further, diverse excuses were offered for no communication with them. As I value a marriage only with the blessings of all concerned where parents have a unique place, I considered them inappropriate.

And quite a few of the candidates, whom I thought to be a prospective match expressed that the bride is either more qualified or placed with a higher pay slab. In one case, the parents of the boy requested me to convince him, but I declined as it would tend to intrude his private space. I could only lament, "The legacy of British India culture still continues, for the females at least. Will their intelligence ever be considered a virtue?" And I yearned for the day when young men and women would treat each other as equal partners and walk on the life's journey side by side, together sharing and caring.

Yet another set of parents or even the candidate asked for the horoscope amongst a number of things and expressed enthusiasm to begin with and a cold response subsequently. I was in a fix. Was there anything wrong? One of my friends who had previous experience explained that in such a scenario, the horoscope of the bride and groom would not have matched for the marriage. And when I asked, 'I deserve an answer, to the least' he clarified that they normally avoid negative information.

In few cases we could not proceed further as the boy looked for only fair complexion. I was reminded of Guruji Rabindra Nath Tagore's writing, "In our land, only fair skinned are considered beautiful. But the sky that radiates light is dark. Glow should come from inner goodness. The virtues and values could put the vanity of world's beauty at shame." I wish the young generation appreciates the wisdom.

There are also a couple of isolated cases, interesting and worth sharing. It depicts a strange human behaviour, which resulted out of necessity or immodesty is beyond my perspicacity. In response to the advertisement, someone telephoned and introduced as the father of the groom and asked to talk to the girl. The request being uncommon, I was surprised and avoided saying that she is otherwise occupied at that moment. I requested for exchanging some details about the bride, groom and family. Instantly, the telephone was disconnected and it increased my suspicion about his intent; but it was beyond my scope to proceed. Two hours after, my daughter picked up the phone and in few minutes she was enraged to remark, "How can I trust you? You started with a lie." She listened for a moment and disconnected with a sharp 'No'. Moments passed in silence. She explained that a man introduced as his father and when she caught him he begged to meet her in Delhi during his visit in next few days.

And in yet another instance, a boy responded to the advertisement sent a dozen SMS and calls without even a preliminary introduction and the language was not palatable. It so happened that with no response from the mobile, he rang on our home land line which I responded. I tried to explain him that it is beyond decorum to disturb others and he should refrain from such inappropriate behaviour. The situation was finally controlled due to a 'total no response' strategy from our side.

As of date, the process is still on. And I feel experienced and inured to cope with. I am however confident that His chronometer would strike a welcome note soon to end the waiting with the emergence of hope; but at times wonder, if the maxim, 'marriages are made in heaven' is true, then why such search/selection trauma? Perhaps, it is the way of His *lila*.

18

Bhim and Bhoi

Be nice to people on your way up, for you never know whom you'll meet on your way down.

—Anon

It was late November afternoon. The market complex of Padampur village in the eastern coast was bustling with people and activity, unlike the November of yester years when quietness pervaded the place and people used to be busy with harvesting and hardly a soul was seen around shopping. Time has since changed. With economy ascending, farming has lost its sheen even in the agrarian rural society. Manual labour to a large extent has been replaced by mechanization. The bullock-carts have been replaced by cycle driven or tractor powered trolleys for transportation of the paddy stock from field to home.

The market has expanded beyond imagination. Since a few years, almost every variety of merchandise traded there. Seldom occasion arises, when one looks for visiting town for procuring things of necessity. Life has become relatively easier. Late afternoon, people stroll around or assemble in groups for chit-chat on the wooden plank in front of some shops whose transactions are limited to daytime. Their talks normally range from social to political, religion to economic, though contemporary news and happenings prevail.

The sun was about to set in the western horizon. Sky was changing its hues and for an astute observer it was really a feast for the eyes. A trolley driver came to enquire from his master, who happened to be in the group if he would make another trip for Arjun as he was pressing to hurry up.

"Don't end up in dark night misdemeanor. I saw brother Bhim, too. He is very particular about safety. I think we'll finish early tomorrow."

"Have you talked to Bhim ?" asked Gouranga.

"No, not personally. I learnt, he has since retired and is back to settle in the village. And Arjun seemed very happy."

Bhim and Arjun are two brothers. As Bhim joined a coveted job, Arjun continued with the family tradition to honour his father's wishes. They are an ideal family: sincere, hardworking, non-interfering and an example in the village.

"He is a source of great strength for all of us." Yogendra said as a matter of fact.

Harihar, a young man trying to establish computer training in the village asked, "We heard a lot about him, his ideals and how he made himself to this stage. Govinda says his son is in US and his daughter is also a professional drawing very good salary in Delhi. Why should he be in this village, then?"

"He always meets us, when ever he is here. In case he has decided to be here, he must have taken a conscious decision. I have seen him grow from penury to prosperity; from a simple peasant's son to a high profile officer in central government. But he is still very simple, sincere and caring." Gouranga continued. "I met his son and daughter about a year back when they were here. You know, his son's salary is a few lakh per month and yet so simple like his father."

Madhukar, a shop owner interjected, "Dr. Mrityunjoy babu is also here for the last few days. His parents are unwell. He too must have retired."

"Oh. Bhoi. They used to be chums: 'Bhim and Bhoi' a sobriquet for Bhim Nath Dhir and Mrityunjoy Bhoi. You know, they studied together, but poles apart: one was from a difficult economic background, the other affluent; one so considerate and caring, the other so arrogant, one so brilliant and the other mediocre."

"In any case he has earned a lot as a surgeon, we learnt." Another interjected.

"Well, earnings are personal. Has he ever thought about others?"

"Bhim bhai has done a lot." Someone added.

"Since his high school days, he has been very active for the welfare of the village. Even in early sixties, he organized a library and reading room in the village.

The high school in the village is due to his pioneering effort."

The discussion that followed reflected a conjecture encompassing strange perceptions arising out of part information – what they have heard, overheard or may have seen out of context and part imagination. The message however was loud and clear: while they had no intentions for invading the private space, their esteem seemed bias towards the benevolent, true to this 'give and take' world.

Some time passed. Night has set in. Darkness hung beyond a few yards of the blazing light of the market. Another person, seeing them in animated interaction announced, "Folks, it is too late for buying vegetables and meeting the home demands. Do have some sense of responsibility." They reluctantly dispersed to the routine; home chore, eat, sleep and wake up to a day of mundane activities.

Arjun also returned via market with a bag full of vegetables and other requisites. He was a bit excited that his brother has agreed to live with them. He went to the area where paddy bundles were to be stacked and arrange for space the next day's arrival. And to his surprise, everything was neatly organized. He could instantly realize that his brother has taken pains to get it done. He proceeded quickly to finish other work and be ready for supper on time.

They talked about the harvest, problem of labour and the wage structure that has rendered the whole agriculture uneconomical. "You must be tired, Take some rest. We'll talk tomorrow." Bhim said.

"Dr. Mrityunjoy (Joy) has come since a few days, I learnt." He informed.

"Have you met him?"

"No, too busy with the harvesting. His parents are also not keeping well. That may be the compulsion."

"I think, I'll meet him tomorrow morning lest he leaves. I'll also pay my obeisance to uncle and aunty."

And they repaired to their respective bedrooms. As the wind rustled the leaves of the trees and the village folks retired for a good night sleep after day's hard work, Bhim tried to close the eyes but wondering thoughts eluded his sleep. On one hand, the inviting reminiscences of the days he spent in the village flashed and on the other he could see his life stretching ahead of him like an endless, bleak and nearly intolerable road by his decision to finally settle in the village leaving his occupation, his inter personal relationship. He tossed and turned and drifted to sleep fatigued.

Birdsong woke him. A pleasant dawn welcomed him for the journey to a new phase of life. There were still a few stars in the clear blue sky. He got ready and biked along the almost deserted path except for the incessant chatter of the birds. By the time he was at the gate of Dr, Mrityunjoy's house the stars have faded and in their place a soft rosy glow heralded immediate sunrise. While he opened the boundary gate, he could feel the uncared for surroundings in contrast to the earlier gaiety. As he entered without waiting for response, powerful memories of the glorious moments came alive. He visualized their golden bond of friendship despite immanent constraints and interests. It was like yesterday that he left for admission in IIT and he was waiting for his selection in the state medical college.

He knocked the door, pushed it open and entered. Though it should have been a homecoming, the absence of usual inviting smile disturbed him. The silence of the languid environment was broken by bouts of cough and he proceeded in the direction. He found the frail body and softly informed, "Uncle, I am Bhim." And he noticed some movement. He tried to face him. As he offered his regards, the strained debilitated voice was audible, "When did you come? Will you stay for a few days or as usual leaving today?" He paused and continued, "It is nice of to have come. I told Joy yesterday to contact you so that I could see you."

"I accepted your advice. I arrived yesterday and think of staying here permanently." He said with supplication.

"How is Arjun? He drops by sometimes."

"He is busy with harvesting. Will meet you soon. Where is aunty?"

"She must be busy with morning chores. She too is unwell. Joy left early morning. He wants me to go with him; but I can't." His weak countenance displayed remorse and the reason was obvious. Without delving into the contentious issue, he tried to console, "You decide what is best for your health and comfort. I'll talk to him."

They chitchatted some time and Mrs. Bhoi joined. Bhim offered his usual *pranam* and helped her to complete brushing and cleaning so that he would take his breakfast and medicine. He assured, "Aunty, please don't worry. Just give a call. I'll be here in fifteen minutes." And departed.

As he biked along, the sun began to rise on the eastern sky. The sleepy village was coming to life and he remembered the way he grew up moving and playing on those lanes, under the shades of the trees, in the sun shine of the farm land and in the shadows of the love and affection of almost all known and unknown. The family's struggle for livelihood, father's perseverance and mother's devotion left indelible mark and he could hardly find anybody to share his feelings with.

He was however not comfortable with the manner his friend has handled the situation. But he thought it proper to discuss when they meet. His own decision to spend the rest of his time here has been troubling him. He did have alternatives and he opted to be here in the village after spending almost four decades in cities here and abroad. "Well, so be it" he concluded and continued with the routine.

Next day, his paraphernalia arrived and he devoted time for arranging them with least disturbance to the existing setup. A few days passed. In the intervening period, many people from the village came to meet him, welcom him and desired to learn his plans. Almost each one has some suggestion that ranged from sharing his knowledge for the benefit of the students to actively guide the village affairs. He was indeed overwhelmed by the feelings expressed.

By the time he was a bit free, he was summoned to attend to the ailing uncle, who was indeed serious. But despite his request, the parents were not in any mood to inform Joy. He had to stop pursuing when he was told, "He has seen my condition. He went for a day. Now it is his wish." As a sincere caretaker, he arranged for doctor and sat beside him praying. Night approached, the peak of activity passed, folks retired. The banal metabolism that maintains life continued undiminished and a peculiar monotonous sound pregnant with foreboding haunted him. His prayer was his only source of strength.

Next morning his younger brother arrived early, to ascertain the seriousness and if he could help. "Aunty, how is uncle?" he enquired.

"Bhim has saved us. He has been awake all through night even without food. He did not listen me, too."

As they entered, they were happy to find the patient well. The face of Mrs Bhoi flashed like a sudden lightening on her remorse laden countenance. Mr. Bhoi expressed his indebtedness. Fighting back tears, she said, "It was so pleasant when the two families used to meet, talk and eat together, sometimes here and at times at your place. And I remember your mother; she was so caring and like my sister would never allow me to do any thing."

It was obvious that she enjoyed the sweet fragrance of the memories reminiscent in her. They helped the old couple get ready and with instructions to the servant departed. They were on their way home. Arjun asked, "Why they are reluctant to inform Joy bhai, who is a doctor himself and could be of great help?"

"Every one of us develops some expectations, particularly from the near and dear ones. If it is seen collapsing, it is a shock. And hope, I am not mistaken, it is their expression of sheer frustration." He continued, "In any case, I am free now and can take care of them."

As a routine either of them visited until his full recovery.

Days passed amidst anxiety and uncertainty: contemplating what lies in store for him. One afternoon, despite the soothing rays of the declining sun in the placid environment he fidgeted under the sun and shade thinking that he has wasted a lot of time and being driven to indolence. By his natural instinct he zeroed to begin a new phase of life and usefully chart an appropriate course. And his attention was drawn to the sound of a vehicle that stopped at the gate. To his surprise, it was Joy who stepped down. They embraced without uttering a word. They met after almost three decades.

As they occupied a cot, he noticed Joy immersed in thought and to break the silence, asked, "Have you come alone? How is bhabiji? Where are the boys now?"

"I am indeed grateful to you for attending to the emergency. "

"They are better now. But you know better the problems of old age."

He explained his problem that he was in no position to stay in this village, as his wife as well as his younger son was unwilling. And that the elder son has postings in Lucknow.

"Are uncle and aunty prepared to stay with you? They would have the benefit of your presence as a doctor." Bhim enquired.

"Neither they are keen to move nor my family would welcome." He said hesitatingly as a confession to a good friend.

His genius of empathy grasped at once the predicament of his friend, a sense of baffled helplessness to choose between what he felt to be the best and what he believed desirable in the circumstances. He could perceive the agony of such a period of painful, precarious living which may be replaced by suffering of being. He needed time to think for a solution that would be acceptable to all.

And before they could discuss further, a few persons came to meet him. He welcomed them and arranged another cot so that they could be comfortable.

"I need not introduce Dr. Mrityunjoy. We have been chums since childhood days."

"We know him." Someone said.

Bhim then explained for the benefit of Joy that since he has arrived he has received enthusiastic welcome and response from the young and old in the village. And that he is grateful to them.

"We have come with some proposals for your consideration." Another responded.

"I am a bit in a hurry. I shall talk to you later." His friend said and proceeded to the gate.

"I think we should think it over and if you could wait a few minutes."

"I am staying overnight. We meet tomorrow." He said while leaving.

Next morning Dr. Mrityunjoy came. He appeared to have spent a sleepless night thinking how to come in terms with a son's duty and a husband's responsibility. He seemed angry because through his life he has only looked after one side and the time has now come that the other aspect need to be taken care of. Like his childhood days, he again came with his problem. Time has changed and the dimension of the problem, but the need for a solution remained.

Bhim invited him for breakfast and he begged excuse. They sat down with tea to continue yesterday's discussion. He broached in, "I appreciate your problem of staying here long. It would affect your professional interest."

"In any case, I am with you. You just tell me what you have decided." He continued.

"The fact is I don't operate at this age. It is a problem of the domestic adjustment. And I need your help."

"Don't worry. I have decided to be here now and would take care of uncle and aunty in the best possible manner. You visit periodically so that they do not feel isolated."

"It is nice of you. And I trust you. But is it proper on my part to evade my duty at a time when it is most essentially needed?" he lamented.

Bhim did not intend to intrude his private space and preferred to remain silent. He diverted to the children. And soon realized that is was a very touching issue as he was not happy with his sons' career. It may be that he has been comparing them with other's children. While he was anxious how to resolve, Joy was deep in thought, reflecting, "A wonderful friend indeed. A man of lion's heart, who courted life with courage, faced calamities with a smile and always ready to help with burning sincerity. And I failed as a son as well as a father."

Noticing his anxious turbulence, he asked, "Hope you are here a few days, Joy?" and with no response, he continued, "We need to accept life as it is and there is no scope for anguish. I have realized, it just does not help as anguish is not a thing of intellect or of the body in isolation." They parted with usual embrace.

Time passed. Sporadic problems of Mr. and Mrs. Bhoi became a cause of concern and Bhim with their consent arranged a physician to regularly visit them and also a nurse for a few hours every morning. The arrangement proved beneficial at least at psychological level. They seemed reconciled. One evening, Bhim asked, "Aunty, hope uncle's worries are reduced to some extent. He looks fine."

And the reply struck him with apoplexy, "In the sunset time of the life he is not much worried about health, but his son's attitude. We wish he learnt a bit from the ideals you set and pursue steadfastly. We perhaps failed to imbibe in him the required values."

19

Technology Adaptation

Far and away, the best prize that life offers is the chance to work hard at work worth doing.

—*Theodore Roosevelt*

Human memory is generally short. The time horizon sometime blurs. But an episode in life's journey that touched heart stay alive and even without the gift of an eidetic memory would flash back on mind's broad canvas in the moments of agony or ecstasy to lighten or enliven. One such incident happened amidst the languid environs of the central secretariat, sometime by the end of last century. The story follows.

It is summer in Delhi. The sun has risen to its noonday peak. An incandescent blinding white in the white hot sky, all colours flat, washed out, stripped off the richness given by the starting light of the early morning. People prefer to be indoors, curtains drawn and at least air coolers on. Schools and colleges too close for vacation. But the bureaucracy is constrained to stick to the approved routine; summer, winter or rain.

The venue is North Block, an important building of the central secretariat that houses the all powerful finance ministry, among others. The magnificence of its grotesque structures that the British constructed to impose their superiority over the ruled has been inherited and utilized by the present day administration. The thick walled, high ceiling rooms offer advantages of sufficient insulation to the heat as much to the society.

A few minutes before 1 pm. The atmosphere inside changes from a serious monotone to brisk activity. Almost every one stops file processing and prepares to break for lunch. Though the official time is 1.30 to 2 pm, by convention it is from 1 to 2 pm. While the officers relax during the break in the air conditioned comfort, the staff rooms being air cooled most prefer to assemble in some cosy corners or go out to participate a *katha* conducted in a cool basements that remain almost idle through the year.

One such day, when *Panditji,* a peon – very important link in bureaucracy but lowest grade in the system-is rushing with two flasks of cold water in two hands for the two rooms assigned to him, a few of his friends face him and ask,

"Why don't you join us for a change?"

"I have a lot of work; to arrange the table for the sahibs and take my tiffin."

"You have memsahib, too to take care of."

"Oh, yes. They take lunch together."

"You have hardly a few years left for retirement. It is time to relax." Someone interjects.

"Please proceed. I'll try some other time." He tries to avoid.

"What do you expect to gain with all sincerity, at this age?" teases another.

"It's my duty. And these sahibs have been so nice to me since I have started working for them. You know, for my son's admission to college, Anita madam expressed to come and help me. And she had to attend a meeting. Annirudha Babu came and completed all formalities. His advice and encouragement inspired my son to the extent that he is determined to be an officer like him."

And they disperse for attending their normal routine. While they are busy with lunch, gossip or *katha,* a bit of historical perspective on how the officers with whom *Panditj*i is attached came into bureaucracy, their assigned role and performance and the like would offer a glimpse of the rumbling that the corridors of power generally witness.

During early 1990s, India faced unprecedented foreign exchange crisis and to tide over the grave situation, government had to pledge its gold in the United Kingdom for foreign exchange to finance nation's essential imports. A parliamentary committee was constituted to find a long-term solution. It recommends a number of ways; some relevant and some not so relevant.

One of the suggestions is to create a special wing dedicated for increasing foreign exchange reserve in the country. The recommendation argues for a professional setup to function independently. It is considered by the committee of secretaries who appreciates the idea and proposes a 'Development Wing' to start functioning in the ministry of finance initially with ten professionals suitable for the job to be recruited with required educational qualification and experience. And it is approved by the cabinet committee for economic approvals and thus acquires the final stamp of authority.

The main source of earning foreign exchange being export which is under the purview of commerce ministry, finance ministry thinks it proper to consult them and finalize the qualification and experience for recruitment. Department of commerce takes serious objection to the proposal: parallel action by another set of officers in another ministry which, it feels, trespassing its jurisdiction. The matter is again reviewed and modified to the extent that the wing in the ministry of finance would be responsible for 'policy, planning, promotion and monitoring' of foreign investment including non-resident investment in India and it would function as 'Investment Wing'.

The ministry decides the structure of the wing. It to have six entry level officers in Group I to be recruited by UPSC and their senior level with two officers from within the ministry and to report to the bureau head who will look after the work in addition to his existing responsibilities. The functioning of the government is indeed complex and paradoxical. The insiders know how to steer a decision and contrive implementation as it suits them. The original decision of an independent wing with professionals gets diluted to induction of only junior level officers and seniors from within. It perhaps reflects their insecurity. Too difficult to conclude.

The process takes about six months and a selected list of candidates approved by the UPSC is forwarded to the ministry. Appointment letters are issued by the ministry for six candidates giving time for taking up the assignment. Finally four officers join.

In the mean time, the physical infrastructure is created. A wing with three rooms for six officers at junior level, two rooms for the two senior officers, a big hall for the section with a section officer, staff, stenos and personal assistants and peons. The rooms are suitably furnished with tables, chairs, sofa, computer, typewriters, telephones, telefax, photocopier and the like as per the entitlement of the officers and the section. The senior officers and the section officer including his staff are pulled from within the ministry and take position. Of the six direct recruited officers, four join and the wing starts functioning.

The head of the division who is asked to look after the work in addition to his normal duties devotes limited time and asks the officers to prepare a plan of action: policy initiative, procedural changes and promotional measures that need to be taken for achieving the goal.

A draft for the plan of action being finalized within the division, the bureau head considers taking the approval of the head of the department and presents it for discussion and finalization. A meeting for the purpose is convened with a few senior officers of the ministry and also from the ministry of industry who are perceived to have knowledge on the subject. As the model plan has been fashioned by the officers joined specifically for the purpose, they present the proposal and provide clarification asked for by the members present. The members find it generally acceptable to proceed and a senior officer expresses satisfaction over the action taken and that the plan is pragmatically designed to begin with, to be suitably modified, if required during the course of operation.

Encouraged by the response, the head introduces the newly recruited officers as a unique confluence of India, four officers coming from four regions of the nation; Annirudha from east, Anita from west, Ayesha from north and Aslam from south. "It is coincidental that they represent four different sects, too" the head informs leisurely over the tea. They all disperse with a happy note: a project implemented.

Time passes. The officers charm their superiors with their intelligence and get appreciation for their sincere efforts. They are simple, sure of themselves, never flustered, always so damn pleasant. The peers and staff appreciate their sweet nature, even temper and a natural dignity.

The implementation of policy and procedural changes towards a more transparent and responsive regime including promotional measures like workshop and seminars conducted in the country and on selected locations in advanced countries show result. Appreciating them for their energy and drive a senior officer on one occasion remarks stoically, "They are the gems on our official diadem that glitter with an almost blinding incandescence against the bleak bureaucratic image painted by a few and perceived by many. And what I like is that they seem to romance with their work."

On the personal front, though they joined the ministry as bachelors, all four of them are married now; but they are best of friends. The intimacy they developed continues which could be attributed to their common background: they have learned values from their innocent parents who tilled their land as their fore fathers and gained peace in life following the social dictum, 'live and let live'. They meet at social level; spend time together, share pleasure and pains. Their bond of friendship grows stronger. And life goes on.

A recent development: they have been assigned to draft a policy document for technology import including indigenous development. Though associated with foreign investment, it is a new subject and they are fully occupied. They discuss the paradigm that involves technology adaptation as against adoption, assimilation and absorption to appropriate technology.

The tiffin munched quickly, they turn to evaluate the status: the extent each has proceeded and required resource to go forward. While they are in the middle of discussion, two of their colleagues enter seeking permission, "Hope, you don't mind our intrusion."

"You are welcome. We too need a respite from the routine" replies one of them.

Though one of them joins for tea, the other has nurtured an intension to gauge their plight in accomplishing the task on a subject the ministry finds difficult. He sees them cool and collected and diverts to something comical. With a flirtatious smile and posture but serious eyes he asks, "I have noted on many occasions including today; your peon sleeping on the long bench with his face covered with a handkerchief. What could be the reason?"

"Well, take it as a puzzle and solve." Ayesha retorts.

"Have you conjectured, since you happen to note it a number of times?" Aslam tries to throw the ball to his court.

"I thought you would have an answer to any such strange behaviour, being in the technology side now." he again attempts to scoff at.

Anirudha senses that the discussion may unnecessarily turn acrimonious and calmly says, "We have been too busy. We hardly find time for such triviality."

"It's now time for tea and he would be here any moment. I think, it is better to ask him and get the answer from horse's mouth." Anita suggests a final solution to end the bizarre talk.

And he punctually arrives with a thermos and arranges tea for all. While all get busy with tea, Anita enquires, "Panditji, why do you cover your face with your kerchief while taking rest after tiffin?"

Intrigued by a sudden and unexpected question he flusters like an examinee in the examination hall seeing questions out of syllabus. He blushes. And to help him, Ayeaha suggests, "Is it the light that hurts your eyes?"

"No, madam. It is to take care of the pollution in the atmosphere." he conjures up.

All flummoxed at the revelation, look askance.

He explains, "The air is too much polluted and I used it as a mask to get filtered air. In your terminology, it could be example for Adaptation of Technology."

Life is a tragedy for those who feel, it a comedy for those who think.
—Horace Walpole

20

Krishna Kali

Life is real, life is earnest and the grave is not its goal.
Lives of great men remind us, we make our lives sublime.
—Longfellow

I woke up and noticed the room filled with blinding light. The digital watch on the side table showed Sunday and 10.21 hrs. It was quite unusual. Maa normally used to take care of things like the curtains drawn, things in order and I maintained routine without fail. I thought, "Has she become suddenly unwell?" and came out of the room. Nobody was seen, not even Pabitra, the maid who used to be ubiquitous from morning till late evening. I remembered I slept with a glass of milk as it was late for dinner and all was well.

I went straight to mother's room and she was not there; peeped into the kitchen where no one can enter without taking bath, and she was not there, too. Surprised, I thought I should better complete morning rituals lest I might be too late. After bath, I went for the normal prayer and it was more surprising that the pooja room lacked its lusture. I concluded something must have been amiss. The unusual quietness as against maa's hyper activity troubled me and my attention was to find bapa. As I have found him always occupied with something engaging, he was couched in a rocking chair on back side verandah and engrossed in reading.

"Where is maa?" I asked.

"Don't worry. She would be back soon."

"But from where?"

"Let's have some breakfast. I was waiting for you."

As the question was avoided, I did not like to probe further. I knew, he would explain calmly.

"Hope you had good night's sleep. I did not wake you up, though your mother wanted me to. She has prepared something. Let's hope, its eatable now." He said as we reached the kitchen. Well aware of his lack of interest in kitchen and cooking, I volunteered to arrange things. He however wanted to help, but I took up the work solo.

"Your presentation is so orderly that it excels a trained chef." were his words of appreciation, while I joined him at the table.

"And my daughter-in-law would be lucky, not as anxious as your mother." He added.

"But where is maa?"

"Well have something. It is nothing serious. She has to go to Pabitra's place."

"Why?" I asked bewildered.

He realized my impatience over the unusual situation that prevailed and continued.

"You know your mother regards Pabitra as her elder sister. She was the young maid attached to her when she came here as a bride and was to take care of the full responsibility of the family. Pabitra not only helped her, but taught her almost all domestic work; procuring vegetables, groceries to cooking, taking care of all of us. And early morning when she was expected, a message came that she has been awe struck and not responding to anyone because her only daughter, Kali is missing. I too wanted to go and console her, but you were sleeping and there is nobody to inform you."

The news was a crude shock to me, too, but I intended not to express any feeling immediately. He gulped a cup of coffee from the thermos and a small piece of sandwich and said, "You take rest. I have to go. If the situation demands, the matter may have to be reported to police. My presence would be required. We'll return soon." and instantly left.

It was past mid-day when my parents returned with Pabitra. Maa consoled her, sent her for bath and hurriedly completed the household chores and a simple lunch for all. A sombre atmosphere prevailed in the house. And we retired to our respective rooms after lunch. I could overhear maa's constant assurance that the girl would comeback and that police has promised to do the needful. But all this could not bring solace to the mother who has lost her grownup daughter. The girl was a few years younger to me and was in the school final. I have heard earlier about her excellent performance in the school.

Next morning usual routine returned except for my mother's cheerful face. While I could appreciate Pabitra's status, but maa's remained an enigma. I waited for the sun to decline so that I could meet my friends. As I approached the meeting point, and tried to duck inside questions and accusations pommelled: 'where were you since yesterday?'

I explained the unusual situation we were in. Even though she worked as a maid, she has been treated as a family member.

"My parents feel it's their duty to support her at such catastrophic moment. And particularly mother is too worried." I informed.

"Your parents are benevolent." A friend mentioned.

Though we enquired about each one's welfare to begin with, the talk centered round the girl. I informed of the faint memory I could recollect about the girl in her young days when she used to accompany her mother, "She was quite sober natured. She would obediently sit down at a place, read and write what my mother has asked her to do. And when I would return home late after cuts and bruises, maa would tease me comparing how innocent and sincere she has been. But since I left for the hostel, I don't think I have had any scope to know more about her."

"I have noted her grow to a pretty young lady. She has an exquisite beauty and anyone who comes across cannot escape being attracted despite her without any garish attire." was the report of another observation.

Jnana, our friend specializing in literature thought for a moment and spoke mildly, "Whether Helen of troy, whose beauty launched thousand ships and burned the topless tower of Ilium really existed is still a matter of some conjecture, but there exists a rival beauty in flesh and blood and it is this girl." He paused and continued,

"She is beautiful as the moon on the horizon, graceful as a cypress that sways in the night wind and glistens in the sheen of a myriad stars. The dimples on her smooth pink cheeks are too pretty indeed. And the charm she reflected smote all hearts to love."

Though we knew of our friend and of his unique talent to paint pictures in words, and excellent style of telling, his narration captivated all of us to think. Another friend asked by way of confirming, "Is she really cute or it is your painting borrowed from Kalidas?"

"I happen to listen to her lilting voice that still rings in my ears." Sarat intoned.

"Hope you are not one of those who mistakes imagination for memory." quipped another.

"Human memory is a treasure house," he said deadpan "and it is only a matter of finding the right key."

While all burst into laughter at his seriousness, his was an innocuous smile in response. I thought, perhaps I missed to appreciate the beauty.

The moon, a barely discernable slice quietly rose through the tranquil sky amid sleepy silence. The night was cool and pleasant and we bade good bye to meet again the next day. While I reached home, a sepulchral silence hung around. It seemed as if a shadow of no living beings stirred: father sat immersed on thought burrows puckered and mother listless. In order to break the silence, I broached in, "I think we should find out from her friends in school and outside whether she has any time in the recent past discussed about any threat from anyone or of her visiting any place with friends and relatives."

"These aspects are taken care of by the police." My father mentioned matter-of-factly.

"The fact is she is young and extraordinarily beautiful. As I have seen her since childhood, she is intelligent, sincere and obedient. I cannot think of that she has left her mother whom she loves so much." my father presented his analysis. What bothered him was that she was not found. As there was no sign of any struggle in the bed, that ruled out application of force. Then where would she be?

Silence fell and it was unbearable. I slipped put of the room and on way to my room, I peeped into the kitchen. Pabitra was preparing something for dinner, perhaps. I thought of offering a word of consolation at a time like this and entered the kitchen. I could not stand the sight of her tear filled eyes puffed red, sleep starved and strained. I venture to say, "Aunty, we all pray God and she would be back soon. Father says, the police is looking seriously. " As she looked to me in response, streams of tears flooded her cheeks.

Her silence spoke volumes. I could scarcely comprehend how a human heart could hold so many tears. A sensitive person could perceive the agony of a mother when her only hope of life, a daughter was missing suddenly.

The next day passed dull with continuous drizzle. I preferred to keep indoors and dozed off after lunch. When I woke from my dreams of being caressed by mother's soft touch, I found her sitting beside me. No sooner I got up, she left without speaking.

An hour or so afterwards I came out of the room and saw Chintamani, on of our elderly workers talking to mother intensely agitated. I overheard him say, "Is it a crime to be born beautiful? It's God's gift. And the poor child suffered all along. She was such an angel; we all miss her, madam." And maa listened to, eyes filled.

The cloudy weather did not allow the sun to induce glamour in the sky. The routine however followed and maa put her evening prayer with *tulsi* lighting wicks. The age old tradition perhaps has been to fight darkness with light as night sets in. Minutes later I entered her room and witnessed the same sombre mood. I intervened, "Everything will be all right. There is no use worrying."

Fighting back tears, she said, "I knew that the poor girl has been tortured by the lecherous rustics to prurient well-to-dos alike; all savouring with lust. While I could have helped, I went on thinking. As a result, I am afraid, she has decided to end her life due to sheer frustration. I feel partly responsible."

We came out as she has to organize the dinner.

During breakfast the next day, I informed that the one week holiday would end in two days and it was time to leave. Then I went father and seeing him alone, asked, "Bapa, why maa is feeling contrite?"

"I have seen her in deep love and care for the kid. I guess, she has developed a fascination for her. The girl was here a day before the incident. Though she shows a bit of trepidation with me, she is quite free with your mother and extends high regards. She informed that she was busy with studies for the exam." I still could not comprehend the total situation, perhaps my limitation. The most disturbing aspect was that of my mother's emotional state: she was as miserable as Pabitra. As far as I gathered, the girl seemed to be lucky to have the love of a hard working mother who toiled to provide her opportunity for education. She being brilliant could get a scholarship for higher studies.

During the lazy afternoon, in a leisurely corner of my room, devoid of any company, not even mother's periodic offer to test something, I recapitulated the observations of my friends, my father's anxieties and Pabitra's silent sufferings over Kali's missing and consolidated the probabilities.

One, a decision to leave at some dead hours of the night deserting the loving and caring mother and being vulnerable to the harsh world is least likely. It could best be a theoretical possibility.

Two, a plan to elope is similarly remote. As I learnt, no one in the school and outside has seen her along with any boy. Such a situation could arise only after a long association, intense love and fear of non acceptance from the parents.

Three, as we have read stories and seen film, bandits picking up pretty women to satiate their lascivous desire or unscrupulous persons kidnapping for flesh trade are also ruled out as there was no disturbance in the bed where she slept along with her mother.

And last but not the least, a stray thought lurked in the minds; has she grown ornery and distant and avoided people? It also occurred to me that she should have gained some courage from the lessons we learn, viz. the story of Cinderella. Such lessons inspire us to face life and in true sense it was her duty to have accepted the sufferings as testing time for God be pleased and usher in happiness.

Even though I had limited association with her during the childhood days, the details I learnt this time has been overwhelming influence: life's journey is indeed very difficult. I looked out into the darkness outside and began to worry, "Who knows what paths her bruised feet trode and what hills of peace or pain she won." And involuntary tears rolled down my cheek.

* * *

Years passed. No information about her whereabouts not even from the police. Pabitra has grown old, but active and continued to stay with my parents. As always, she has been a good company for my mother and a helping hand. As a professional, my placement has been in the metro city, Bangalore where my parents were delighted to visit, but not inclined to stay. Though I have been feeling it's my duty to take personal care of them at their advancing age, my daughter's education and my job assignment on the other side, seemed not in coeval. I thought of deciding at an appropriate time and waited for His direction.

Once I was coming home with wife and a ten year old daughter by train. The night passed well in the air-conditioned comfort and we had breakfast. In a small station, a saffron clad woman entered, enquired a seat number and asked her two companions to leave.

"I'll get down the next stop. It's about an hour and half journey. I'll not disturb you." She said.

Her voice in soft cadence and the smile that created a fissure on her smooth cheek enhanced her ascetic beauty.

"You have a right to your seat and we welcome you. I would be benefited by your company, as he (my husband) keeps himself engrossed in books and I have started feeling lonely." my wife replied. They chitchatted for sometime and I could witness an unusual closeness developed instantly.

"Next stop, where I'll get down is our ashram. When you return, please stop by for a few hours and you will see our endeavour. You'll certainly like, I assure." She extended an invitation and handed over a small booklet.

"Everyone at the station knows about us. They are quite co-operative and would not charge extra for your transport." She added.

It was my wife's turn. How could she be lagging? She promptly replied, "We would love to be your guest and see your activity, but you have to join us and visit our home. Please do come along with us. My in-laws would be too happy to meet you."

And to my surprise, she readily agreed. When a person came to receive her she calmly informed, "I'll return in a day or two. Please inform baba. Some urgent work, which I shall explain on return."

We had another few hours journey to reach our destination. My daughter was still sleeping. I became curious to study their activity.

"The person, who came along, addressed her as 'Gurumaa'. She looks so beautiful and of my wife's age, in early thirties. What has driven her to an ascetic life?" I wondered.

I preferred to keep my curious enquiry to myself and continued with my book. When my wife informed that she has agreed to be our guest, I formally welcomed her.

"My parents also believe in a sacred life and you'll not have any difficulty." I said.

While I continued wondering at their instant relationship, they talked. In the mean time, my daughter also woke and was introduced to her. She too fell in love with her charm and I reminded that she need to complete washing and take something as the time is approaching for our destination.

"I'll take with grandma. Let me have some time with aunty."

"You will have enough time to talk to her. She has agreed to be our guest for a few days."

"Oh, that's great." She said in exhilaration.

We alighted from the train when sun began to decline from its mid-day peak.

"Life in a small town is really pleasant." I said on way home.

"Please see our ashram. It's spread over a vast natural landscape on the bank of a river. Its serene atmosphere will boost your spirit."

"What are your activities?" I asked out of sheer curiosity.

"Though regular spiritual discourses are conducted, usual to any ashram, the important activity is maintaining a home for the aged men and women, who by circumstances or choice are deprived of love of the near and dear ones."

"It's novel. But you are so young, and your associates called you 'Guruma'." I posed.

Before she could respond, we arrived at our home.

The day for us was usual rest, eating and talking. My friends of the young days being scattered to earn their bread, I thought of interacting with our guest and take her around along with my daughter.

I asked my wife to enquire her willingness and suggested evening time is better to go around, depending on her choice out of the few options here.

My wife stayed back to help mother and we started as scheduled. She showed her enthusiasm visiting a new place.

"How should I address you?" I asked politely.

"You should be older to me. Please call me Bhabani. It's the name I owe to my baba."

When I posed the same query I wanted to know while on way home from the station, she preferred to be philosophical, "It's a long story and I'll not bore you with. You know we as ship wreck sailors floating in the life's stream. Some are fortunate to get a shelter and some keep on trying through out life. I feel fortunate to have the blessings of baba. You will meet him at the ashram."

I had no option but to agree and complimented her for dedicating to a noble social cause at this age. "As I mentioned, I appeared in the scene when baba has become old. He still guides. And I have taken the challenge to pursue his dreams actively, of course with his support." She clarified.

Next morning, I saw her in the kitchen along with my wife and despite request not to take trouble as a guest, she said, "Hope you would not deny me the honour of serving once."

Her keen interest to accept invitation to be a guest

in strangers place, her respect and care for my parents including Pabitra puzzled me. I decided to focus a sharp attention on her. When the preparation for the lunch was appreciated by all, mother informed that it has been prepared by her. And my daughter asked, "You cook such nice dishes daily at ashram?" "No, my child. Life at ashram is different." Her tone was laden with emotion.

When we were sitting outside in the late afternoon, she came with tea tray and Pabitra some recipe, prepared by her.

My mother was feeling uneasy that she, as a guest was being troubled. And suddenly, she explained for the benefit of my parents, "We are successfully running a home for the old at our ashram and we have arranged funds for another. I think a place in the vicinity of this town would be suitable. And I can expect some help from you."

As my father looked askance, she clarified, "We don't ask for money. If you can devote some time, we shall be grateful."

"I don't know exactly how I could be of help to you, at this age?"

"Oh uncle, you are as fit as a fiddle. You will be a great asset for us. I'll also come a few days every week to support you."

I could see a brilliant glow in my father's eyes as he saw it as an opportunity to engage himself. A brave new world was springing up like a neat *Lego* model built from assorted components. We discussed some locations and how to obtain Government's accent to the project. The following morning, Bhabani decided to leave.

"Though I feel like continuing here till death under the shadow of love, duty calls upon me to leave. In any case, I'll be there to pick you up tomorrow. Please spend sometime with us. We shall be honoured. And you will get an idea what we do." She told my wife.

"Please do come again, *beti.*" Pabitra requested.

"We are going to establish another ashram here. I'll keep coming to trouble you, maa."

She replied unctuously and looked to the other side in the car.

When I returned seeing her off at the station, Pabitra was ecstatic. But she did not express openly. Sometime during the day, I discussed the matter with my mother and she also endorsed my conjecture.

Next morning when we were to leave, my parents and Pabitra came to say 'good bye' and offer their blessings. And when the car was about to start, Ppabitra came close to the car window by my side and humbly requested, "*Beta,* you are going to the ashram. Please ask her and confirm me that she is my 'Kali', my 'Krishna Kali'."

While my father stood agape at the sudden revelation and I was at my wits end. And my wife, unaware of the past was petrified. Surprisingly, mother became emotional and anxious. She probably felt what Pabitra has expressed. As we moved physically to the station, my mind raced at jet speed to flash back the scene: traumatic experience of my mother and Pabitra when kali was not found. I wondered whether it could be a mother's overt love or brazen reality. And thought it wise to leave for the time to decide!

21

Bibhuti

To see the world in a grain of sand
And heaven in a wild flower,
Hold infinite in the palm of your hand
And eternity in an hour. —*William Blake*

PART ONE

Bibhuti, a Peasant's Son

A journey of a thousand miles begins with a single step.
—*Confucius*

The Hamlet God's creation is infinite and the universe is enormous. Amongst the billions of galaxies in the universe, there exists a small galaxy called 'Milky way' clustered with trillions of stars. One of its small stars is the sun and our planet Earth rotates around it with its rhythm. Science has mapped the development. The cosmological theory: 'Big Bang' a unique cosmological splendour happened about five billion years ago. The universe was filled with diffused clouds of gas at extraordinarily low entropy level. Mutual gravitational attraction of its constituents caused the primodial gas to clump and after a billion years, the clump ultimately formed galaxies, stars and the lighter and small ones the planets. The low entropy source of energy allowed low entropy life forms to evolve. A miracle!

The earth is unique because it sustains life. It is divided into continents, countries, cities, hamlets, buildings with many floors and huts made of clay and straw. Orissa, a small state is on the eastern coast of India. It is hemmed in by the Bay of Bengal on the east, guarded by mountain range in the south west and opening to the northern plain. The state has an enchanted past and inviting future. In the fabled past, poised mid way between dream and reality, the land - *Utkal Janani* washed her hair in the Ganges and rinsed her feet in the Godavari. She has been identified as Udra Desha in Mahabharat, Oretes by historian Pliny, Wu-cha by the Chinese traveler Hiuen Tsang, Udra Vishu by Alberuni. History apart, the names Udra, Utkal and Kalinga still weave magic in the living memory of the people of the land. The modern Orissa however was born on the 1st April, 1936.

The state comprises mostly with villages of the pre independent India, the culture in its essential elements continues to exist even today where seasons are marked by festivals and ceremonies, where stages of life are punctuated by family and community rituals, where eating and routine life of work for man folk and cooking, sleep, gossip for women, where hard work is rarely divorced from the rhythm and where neither power nor profit has precedence over an easy going life.

One of the many hamlets is Shivpur, the name borrowed from *Shiva* enshrined in the ancient temple and worshipped by one and all, believed to be the only saviour. It resembled the neolithic village where the family, the neighbours and the friends are all parts of a visible, tangible, face-to-face community. Most of the villagers inescapably attached to the land, destined to live and die in a pre modern agrarian society scrabbling at the unyielding soil as their ancestors did centuries ago. And number of cows, bullocks, bullock-carts, fields of paddy, silos and labour employed determined the status of a family.

The houses are of mud walls and thatch roof, generally on rows extended per necessity as a result of division among brothers over generations. The upkeep of the house is taken care of by the womenfolk who apply a thin layer of special clay and cow dung every morning. Thorough cleaning is normal twice a year for every household; once after sowing for the festival *raja sankranti* and another after harvest for *maker sankrati*. In addition similar cleaning is undertaken to sanctify after any death or birth and also for special celebration like marriage.

March is usually transit period from winter to summer, the official spring season. It is the most pleasant period of the year with slightly cool night, and moderately warm day. Usually during early March every year, *Shivrarti* the auspicious occasion of the union of *shiva* and *shakt* is celebrated with gaiety. It is the annual fair for the village. The day begins with the roosters' crow when people gather near the temple site spread between the temple and the great pond of the village. The four sides of the pond have rows of mango, palm, banyan and other tropical fruit trees. The villagers occupy a small space each in a row on the boundary line for the ladies to sit through night and light the holy lamp in honour of the supreme deity and the sellers on the other side to spread their merchandise. After a long hour of pre dawn activity they clear the area and leave. By sun rise the priest consecrates his body (mind?) with a dip in the great pond and proceeds to the temple chanting *'Om Namah Shivaya'* partly to announce his arrival and partly to meditate on the presiding deity. The devotees, mostly ladies arrive with plates full of flower, fruits, milk, sugar, *bel* leaves and incense sticks fasting to pray and place before God their wish list for fulfillment. The day long worship continues and by afternoon, people from neighbouing areas would also join to buy, sell, meet friends, eat, enjoy and of course to pay obeisance.

The main activity is during the night. The women sit in their temporary hut and light lamp that continues till morning. During the night most of the womenfolk who have struggled for savings during the year would come to buy cosmetic materials and fancy items which the sellers have procured from the city Calcutta, the men procure home utilities and the children spend the amount received from the elders on small toys and eatables.

His Birth

It was the day of *Shivrarti* in 1945. The eastern sky was iridescent signaling sunrise and the cool morning breeze filled the atmosphere with the aroma of the spring flowers. The placid village had bustled with activity: the men and children of the village gathered around the *Shiva temple* busy arranging a small place for the respective family and women preparing for fasting and prayer. The family of Fakir was busy otherwise; one member hurrying to invite the doula to take care of the delivery. A village at that time had no scope for a paramedic what to speak of a qualified nurse or doctor.

By wont, the doula, the mother and the mother-in-law were with the expectant mother (*bahu*). Others in the family and near relatives were waiting in anticipation. Anxious moments passed because Durga had in two previous occasions lost the baby during delivery. "On this auspicious day, by His grace I am fortunate to have a grandson." the voice of the mother-in-law was heard. "Pay obeisance to the Divine. Blow a conch in honour of *Shivji.*" mother supplicated. And a wave of ecstasy swept over the family and friends with the first cry of the baby.

Deliberations continued for a few days for naming the boy. The maternal grandfather being the eldest had the honour and he chose 'Bibhuti', the sacred ash which *Shiva* smeares over his body and a divine *prasad* for the devotees. "The boy is a precious gift from Him for the family and the society." he declared.

Childhood

The reminiscences of the childhood are always a source of great pleasure and sometimes exciting even in the background of a rural penurious life as one tends to compare with the subsequent stages laden with duties and responsibilities. Bibhuti always described his childhood days as halcyon passage. He was born at a time when there was no child in the extended family that lived physically separate but emotionally bonded. There were grandmas, uncles, aunts, cousin sisters and brother, all of them were adults. Surprisingly he was too contented; feed on mother's milk, sleep, smile and play. While the sisters expected that the baby should cry and they would be called upon to take care of, they were disappointed. Envious of everybody's showering of love and affection for the boy, they would tell all, known and unknown, "Oh, what a funny child. He doesn't even cry." And in reply any grandma present would quip, "He is blessed to laugh and make others laugh, too. Why can't you understand?" The cousin brother however was happy to sit by, play with and enjoy the company.

One of the uncles in the extended family used to stay only with his mother, a grandma for Bibhu. And it was the place where he used to spend most of the time when his mother was busy with household chores. As he started crawling, he started helping her by driving away the crows or picking up a piece of wood for the fire. Time passed and he started learning alphabets and numbers with a slate and chalk that the uncle had gifted.

School Days

The village had a primary school and happened to be in proximity to his home. By the time he was four years, the headmaster of the school thought he was old enough for attending school. And he was admitted. The change of the routine from eating and playing to the responsibility of regularity, punctuality and sitting upright long at a place bothered him only few days and there was no looking back. True to his head master's dictum, '*a basil plant is known from two leaves*' within days he became a blue eyed boy of the teachers, peers, neighbours including the family and relatives. They predicted from the first that he was brilliant and going to the top of the tree. He received more attention and recognition for his intelligence, diligence and sincerity. He proved securing scholarship in lower primary stage (standard III) and primary level (Standard V).

Even as a child he was very sensitive to the family conditions particularly the hard labour put in by the parents to meet both ends. He too liked a modest living style with no demand and helped the parents in any manner possible. He was satisfied with what ever food available, a short and a shirt for the school and minimum requirement of the school paraphernalia: text books, paper to make copies, ink-tablets for ink and a pen. By the age of about eight he started helping his father during the trying times of cultivation, ie. sowing and harvest. He also took keen interest in playing in leisure times, swim across the big pond of the village and moving around with friends.

On an occasion he emotionally conjured up, "A half a century ago, life was different. It was jungle all around; full of tropical fruit trees, on the sides of the village pond, in agriculture land, on road sides, in everyone's premises and spread deep further. The seasonal flowers, bird songs filled the languid atmosphere. People were generally seen happy even amidst scarcity. And we were a group of about five or six, normally on a rendezvous every afternoon after school. The tastes of the fresh and juicy fruits still sweeten."

By this time a middle school (Standard VI & VII) started functioning in the village and he continued with study. The new school was located at one end of the village. It had only one teacher for two classes and

English was the new language to be studied which required additional time to cope with. The students were to attend classes after the normal school timings. In addition to study, they also carried water for drinking from a well a few furlongs away and help the teacher in cooking. About two months before the examination they used to stay in the school at night to concentrate and get by heart a few important answers for passing the examination. The school was almost their home during the period. And as usual he appeared in the scholarship examination as a nominated student of the school. But as luck would have it, the result of the examination was not declared by July, the admission time for High School.

The other factors that had lasting influence on his life include: first, there was no high school in the village and the cost involved to stay in hostel for study was considered prohibitive for the family; second, a boy in the neighbourhood in standard VIII joined army to the dismay of his family, relatives, neighbours and it was construed that any one going to high school may have an easy option for such misdemeanor; and last but not the least middle school pass met the eligibility criteria for a teacher's job in a primary school, sufficient for a living. The cumulative effect was catastrophic. He could not join any high school to continue studies. The result came by December with scholarship in his favour but it was of no avail. Though a vain attempt was made for admission, for it was too difficult to deny to a scholarship-holder, but the earlier considerations prevailed and he suffered a 'torture of hope'. The people who liked him most like, the maternal uncle, elder uncle held series of discussions to find ways that he continued his studies but they being economically worse could not help finding any solution. And he was fated to discontinue study and get engaged in tilling the land which his fore fathers did and continue to lead the life of a poor peasant.

The joy of life, it seemed,. had gone. The past relegated to oblivion and the horizon in every direction bleak, he was forced to live in the ceaseless present: eating and sleeping at home, assisting father when required and otherwise totally alone, crying in isolation and reflecting, "What alternative do I have? I am only eleven and by the time I would be eligible to apply for the post of a primary teacher it is yet another ten years and I would have forgotten what I have read."

He started living in the shadow of uncertainty and gloom. The change was perceptible to all; friends, neighbours and equally to those who loved or envied him. All missed his infectious smile, ubiquitous presence and ever ready to sincerely devote for any errand he was asked to take care of. He was just missing from the scene. To him the world was not born anew everyday as it used to be. The morning sun, the sweet breeze, the picture perfect horizon seemed mundane, listless.

One evening his elder uncle completing his usual rituals came in search, "Bibhu, where are you? Pray you are well. Why are you not coming even to our side? Come, see. What have I got for you?"

Fighting back tears, he would come and stand by his side without a word. And his elder uncle was at great pains to express his inability to do something to bring back smile he rightly deserved. He offered him his favourite sweets and sympathised, "Don't loose heart. He is great and will certainly do what is good for you. Keep faith." And left emotionally hurt. He too went inside to shed some more tears over the fate that divine scripted to be endured.

Then came the harvest time; the busiest period for the farmers to consolidate that would take them through the year. And for Bibhuti a new beginning: to be groomed for the full time occupation of a peasant. While he tried to get absorbed in the profession, words of sympathy from the known and unknown pummelled. Though their intention was to share their feelings for someone deprived, it rent his heart. The sombre winter passed and spring came as usual with all its bounty but could not bring him cheers. He would awake to the day and reflect, 'I wake and feel the fell dark, not day.'

Marriage

Springtime though transient, offers many advantages for the agrarian society: temperate climate, plenty of local vegetables, after harvest leisure time and some money for fun and frolic. The period is considered optimal for elaborate celebration like marriage when relatives, guests are entertained for a long time. Those days child marriage (marriage of pre-pubertal bride) used to be very common as it was believed that the parents offering a bride (*kanyadaan*) would certainly ascend to heaven. And this marriage would finally be consummated when the bride attains puberty in a similar ceremony laden with rituals on an auspicious day.

It was the year Bibhuti passed middle school. The decision of two of his friends' marriage was discussed by friends and neighbours with great enthusiasm, but it could hardly evoke any excitement in him as he was still caught in the anxious misery; round and round and round. He couldn't fulfill his dream, his yearning for higher studies.

Despite the fact that his friends were well aware of his mental and emotional condition, they dropped by one afternoon asking him to join them during a visit of one of their classmate for a chat about his marriage. Reluctantly he agreed to and while they met he presented him a couplet:

And when you are married,
O, how happy you'll be;
For, you would love her
And she would love you.

And for his friend the piece of paper is still a priceless possession. Suddenly, after a few days, like a bolt from the blue he heard the discussion about his marriage being finalized. 'A unique moment in one's life.' And that moment seemed to bend him inexorably downwards. Without realizing he began to drift as if his roots have been pulled, as if he were floating down a river and struggling to hold a side branch. He grew very ornery and distant. 'Grief turnout to be a place none of us know until we reach it. We anticipate shock, not to be obliterative and dislocating both to body and mind.' And thus struck catastrophe.

While he used to weep to himself with consolation that he was born in a poor family and had no means to advance; 'it is all destiny. What is ordained will happen and I'll have to contend with being a poor peasant.' But the decision about his marriage shattered him. He cried, begged before parents, relatives and well-wishers to spare him from the avoidable torture at least for some time. And to his surprise, even those who sympathized with him for higher studies saw no problem in marriage and cited examples of his two friends getting married soon.

Desperately he needed someone to talk to, someone to share with who would appreciate his feelings. He tossed, turned and fidgeted through out the night sleepless. When he came out the stars have faded and in their place a soft rosy glow heralded immediate sunrise. The night breeze has quietened. He moved aimlessly and drifted to an isolated direction. The long shadows of the morning gradually reduced. As he walked along, a woodpecker was perched on a gnarled branch knocking at the trunk in search of water, a crane flew by its moon-white wings gleaming against the azure sky and a small snake glistened, slithered around and disappeared. 'Are these bad omens?' he thought, but could hardly find interest to follow.

'Time is a great healer.' Though the decision of marriage has shattered him, deprived him of the childhood too soon like an accident, the routine that followed mired him to life of a peasant. Consequent on consistent coaxing and cajoling, naively with a trusting lamb-being-led-to-slaughter acquiescence he finally decided to accept life as it is and live it fully. He was married to an innocent looking pretty girl without any education. Now, about half a century later, with some insight to the scriptures he could rationalize the philosophy of marriage, *"Bride yearns for beauty, her mother for wealth, her father for learning, relatives for family honour and the rest for a feast."* And there is no scope for the groom and his wishes. How true indeed!

His parents perhaps took a decision which they perceived appropriate to their mundane background ignoring its long term effect and what he has to endure. True to his nature and ardent faith he reflected, "He sometimes gives paper and pencil for writing and sometimes spade to work in the field." The hurt lingered as he craved for the halcyon passage of the childhood, while duty demanded work in the field. And gradually he started getting inured to cultivation as a profession.

barely sufficient to sustain life and the inmates depended on the stock of perched/puffed rice for morning breakfast they get from their home periodically with exception of a few who could buy *parothas* and sweets from a local vendor. And in the event of continued monsoon rain or other exigencies, the rest solely depended on the principal meals.

Regular 10 am to 4 pm classes continued as per the school routine. The subjects seemed interesting; but he had to fight against homesickness and problem relating to keeping pace with peers. With difficulty, he managed to procure a few books that the seniors advised as a requirement for the four year term and for the rest he had to be content to depend on friends for their availability. After about three months, the school broke for pooja holidays and one and all went home. And on his arrival, almost all his friends, well-wishers including teachers came to bless him success and advised to study hard to keep the flag flying. To one of his friends he told,

"I find poverty is a curse. I don't even have a few shorts and shirts to put on occasions. Some of my classmates exuded high degree of self confidence, intelligence and talent. They looked fit and perfect. Are they the children of affluence? Are they, like me trying to rise from obscurity and poverty but possess an innate strength to go to the height? While I don't have any information, I do certainly feel lost."

One of his teachers heard of his agony and consoled,

"You have the right to study sincerely and just do that. Leave the rest to Him. I am sure you'll succeed."

He followed the advice and his inner voice. Though not sophisticated and cosmopolitan in attire, his great presence in the class room, in competition, organizing events and finally in the result of the examination, he outshone his contemporaries and it put all the speculation to rest. No one in the class was near him in any subject. Though the limitation due to unavailability of trained teachers had telling effect on the board result, games like foot-ball and volley-ball, sometimes drama and debate, and occasional programme of picnic provided additional avenues for enjoyment in addition to the students' secret indulgence. He once told me, "Everyone expects a little excitement, avenues to show talent. It is not proper that only city-bred have the franchise on all enjoyment." During the four tumultuous years of the high school, certain events like walking fourteen kilometers from home to school in a group during vacation, talking of bizarre experiences, stories and jokes for a lively time and to fight fatigue made an indelible mark.

He vividly remembered, "I'll certainly describe a few occasions the memory still covets: first, when we used to walk in groups to visit some carnivals almost twice a year during the first three years, final year fully devoted to preparation for the board examination; second, a week long strike in the school on a trivial issue like digging the well deeper for availability of drinking water and third, the fate of a cunning person as our headmaster."

"Well, there were not any special festivities or fair in the vicinity of the school, not even a good market. But at a distance of about five-seven miles, there used to be very popular fairs: once a year the village would flare into transient brightness for a day or two, may also extend a few days if some open-air opera visited. The crowd would then disperse, vendors pack off and the fair is gone. The warmth fades like a shower in midsummer leaving barely a trace. The village returns to its tranquil state. But for us the enthusiasm starts with the idea of visit, planning, walking in a group through the tropical pleasance feasting on the scene: the barefoot boys, cowherd, hen with its chicks and thatched huts interposed against the background of forest. And when finally at the fair site the chanting, shouts, noise and people of all ages craning for a glimpse of what that could be inside the group gathered and so engrossed. Such groups were everywhere for selling, showing some magic and even for advertisement. We too roam around for an overview. Tired and thirsty, most of us could hardly afford a *sarbet* to quench our thirst. Usually we would return discussing items that appealed to each. Sometimes in a pensive mood if one would retrospect on the pain and gain from such a visit, the only plausible answer could be: a change from the routine."

He continued, "Though the visit was avoidable luxury, driving a situation for a strike was perhaps unavoidable. I was in Class IX. As the summer ensued the water scarcity became very critical. A small well, not so deep could not meet the drinking water requirement of the school and the hostel with about eighty students. We discussed with the school secretary of the management committee who had the authority and finance. Our request was simply to dig the well a bit more so that sufficient drinking water would be easily available. But the inaction of the management evidently showed disregard to the basic need. And one day just after the meal at 9 AM, I with the support of a few friends and the tacit approval of the teachers made an ethereal speech for adopting the Gandhian principle and leaving the school, abandoning class so long the well is not dug enough and drinking water is available. It appealed all and in half an hour the whole hostel was deserted. The attendance was limited to the day-scholars who were very few and therefore the school was declared closed."

He paused, fought back tears and intoned, "The management took action, but perhaps under duress. The well was dug deep enough for a better source of water that carried us through. When we returned friends congratulated me for the victory and teachers patted me in private. I was torn between gratitude and action: gratitude because I owed the management the offer of scholarship that enabled me to continue my study and such drastic action as a result of the indifferent attitude of the management towards, what we thought, our trivial request for a basic need. In any case the outcome was too revealing. I learnt from a source close to the secretary that he asked the headmaster to rusticate me for indiscipline and the move was thwarted by none other than the headmaster himself, offering to resign and leave in the event of such inappropriate action. It was indeed an eye opener as to what people really value. Ignoring the feelings we thanked the teachers and the management for their benevolence."

He further added, "The difference between the secretary and the headmaster continued and widened. By the beginning of the next session, the headmaster decided to leave and we are left guardian less.

Time passed at its own pace and we suffered for want of trained teachers who could guide us. The management appointed another headmaster who claimed to be B.A. B.T., equivalent to B. A.B. Ed. He projected himself a true disciple of Vinoba Bhave, who was a very popular, leading nation wide *'Bhudaan Andolan'* for equitable distribution of land among the landless in peaceful manner. His attire was hand woven *khadi dhoti*, *khadi* scarf and wooden sandal. He continued with the subjects taught by the previous headmaster and English in our class. The initial few classes were for his assessment about our knowledge in English. As the new topic started, we had a lot of questions for clarification and to our surprise he only asked us to write without explaining. It continued for some time. In the mean time one of our friend told that one of his cousins was a B.T. after high school and is teaching in a primary school. We instantly concluded that our present headmaster must be similar. And I was to inform the secretary.

One evening after the class, I reached and found some members of the management busy in discussion. With trepidation, I paid my obeisance, "Good evening, Sir."

"Well, any fresh problems that bother you or you have come to serve notice of another strike?" the secretary retorted.

"No sir, this is a very serious matter and I want to talk to you personally."

"Ha, Ha, Ha talk to you in private...no, never. You may tell all of us. They are all well wishers of the school."

Before I could gain composure for a reply, the previous secretary of the school asked, "You should listen to him and then decide. In case you have problem, let me handle this."

"You are not aware how he forced a strike in the school last year. He is too smart."

"Well, as my son informed me, you people are responsible for such a situation."

The secretary felt embarrassed to argue further and called me to another room. I bowed in supplication and moved to an empty room where we both stood.

"Sir, the present headmaster is not a trained graduate. His knowledge in English is poor." I vomited.

"Oh, yes, yes. You are the only learned person and all others including your teachers have little knowledge."

"I thought it my duty to inform you, what we all feel." I said and came out. The previous secretary called me and said, "We'll certainly consider your request. Please devote to studies. The school expects a lot from you."

I thanked him and left.

The headmaster continued to take our class in English and the students who never dared to even speak started asking questions without any specific reply. We were gradually more convinced that he is not what he claimed but could do nothing. After about a month, one day the secretary came and asked him to give the certificates of all teachers required to be submitted to authorities for the recognition of the school. While the other teachers complied he informed that the certificates were at his native place. The secretary requested him to immediately get, as it was very urgent. The next day he left for home and to the surprise of all he did not return. And we suffered for want of the English teacher." The next year, Class XI for Bibhuti also passed with some temporary arrangement.

All is well that ends well. The result of the state secondary board examination surprised all; the friends and foes alike. He came out in flying colours securing a place in the gallery of 'best ten students' in the state. A unique honour. It was a climactic moment and he was in elements. There was exultation amongst friends, relatives, teachers, neighbours, school and the society. By His grace, a national level scholarship was introduced for meritorious students for higher study and he was a recipient.

"The events though very important one time, remains only as an incident in life. This is but natural." He philosophised.

In College

We mortals are not capable of appreciating His *leela*. It is proved here once again: Bibhuti no doubt suffered the trauma of discontinuance of study for one year, but for a greater purpose. He continued higher education with the support of the scholarship without which it would have been impossible. And the scholarship was announced just prior to the announcement of his high school result. A strange but true coincidence. The value of the national scholarship was sixty rupees per month during undergraduate level and he decided to manage with, as he had never forgotten the habit of austerity learnt since childhood from parents who both because of necessity and principle lived a spartan life.

In the mean time, his young wife has attained puberty and his in-laws proposed a ceremony for the consummation of the marriage in tune with the canons of the social order. Some relatives envious of his overwhelming success too exerted pressure, but his parents stood firm on continuation of higher studies and postponement of the ceremony. Though it was a point of debate for some time, in the interest of providing impetus to the prospects of higher studies for a bright student good sense prevailed.

The best college in the state would have welcomed him to join, but he preferred to attend the nearest college. Penury was the compelling factor. The elegant symmetry of the mathematics and the pristine logic of science drew him with an almost magnetic force to the science discipline. He was admitted to the Pre University Science class. Soon he realized that he will receive the scholarship only by the later part of the session and it was uphill task to manage college fees, hostel fees, books and other paraphernalia with limited resources at his disposal. It was a catch 22 situation. It was no easy task to exit from the impasse. He, in the circumstances spent only for the essentials. He was among the limited few to attend class with shorts instead of trouser. Owing to outstanding academic performance the students wanted to consult him for any doubt and teachers couldn't ignore. As his excellence, so his attire attracted everyone's attention. Though it was his compulsion, the affluent could hardly appreciate. He once described the incident, with eyes filled reflecting how agonized he was.

"A lecturer in a tutorial class made an oblique remark, because he considered it obscene for the grownup college students to attend class with shorts. I had no alternative but to swallow the insult, but pondered over a long time as to why even educated people are unable to appreciate others limitations. The matter however reached the principals office and very soon in a meeting of all students and faculty a senior professor stated, "It is for the information of all staff and teachers of this college that college education is no longer the monopoly of the affluent few as it used to be during the British Raj. The teachers need to attune their attitude and encourage all, particularly the deserving and meritorious students belonging to economically backward strata of the society." He later called me and consoled. He also advised me to forget the incident, concentrate with studies. The issue no doubt was put to rest, but I remained emotionally hurt."

Despite racked with agonizing pain handicapped by financial constraints, he followed the advice and his inner voice. Though not sophisticated and cosmopolitan in attire, his great presence in the class room, in competition, organizing events and finally in the result of the examination he outshone his contemporaries and it put all the speculation to rest. He improved his performance in the final university examination of Pre University Science and was also selected in the much coveted IIT Entrance securing admission at the most prestigious IIT. He ventured to join and realized within a month of stay that the expenditure involved was far more than the scholarship he would receive. He found it was beyond his scope and returned back to the same college to study in Pre Professional Science class. His inexorable travail continued. He secured first rank in the university. He became an example and source of inspiration for many students who pursued for excellence. All those who knew him personally adored him. He enjoyed a celebrity status and continues to have a respectable place among the alumni even to date.

University Education

He learnt from a senior student of the college who graduated in engineering that there was a scheme for toppers to join directly in the second year in IIT including Benaras Hindu University and at Benares the cost of living including fees would be well within hundred rupees a month. The information was exciting: it was within his means and his dream for a respectable profession would be realized. He applied for admission. On receipt of a telegram for admission to the second year class he arrived at Varanasi Railway station on a cloudy morning of early July, alone.

On his way from Calcutta to Benares, he learnt that Varanasi, Kashi and Benares are the same holy city of *Shiva* where myriad faithful arrive for departure; to die and burnt in a legendry *'burning ghat'* and ashes dissolve in the Ganga, to escape the remorseless cycle of birth-death-re-birth, to get away to eternity. Richard Lennoy wrote, "Living among the people of this extraordinary city opened my eyes to levels of psychological and spiritual awareness which we in the west, with our most externalized preoccupations had thrust into the unconscious. Benares has a way of persuading one to comfort hidden, but universal, human proclivities. This is especially apparent in the city's unflinching attitude to morality."

He subsequently learnt that the name, Varanasi has been derived from the geography of the sacred city, most particularly the area between two small rivers that flow into the Ganga: Varan in the north and Asi in the south. It was also enchanting that the lanes of the city and *ghats* on the Ganga have been treaded by the great saints Buddha, Mahavira, Sankaracharya and great poets Tulsi Das and Kabir to mention a few. Reverend M. A. Sherring (1868) wrote, "Benares is a city of no mean antiquity. Twenty five centuries ago, at the least, it was famous. When Babylon was struggling with supremacy, when Athens was growing in strength, before Rome had become known, she had already risen to greatness. While many cities and nations have fallen into decay and perished, her sun had never gone down; on the contrary, for long ages past it has shone with almost meridian splendour." And his journey to this city of learning was to gain education.

Life to begin with was no honky dory. He joined a class of sixty students who have studied first year in engineering and for him the subjects like drawing, engineering mathematics, applied chemistry and physics in addition to workshop were totally new. Usual ragging in hostel also took its toll. While his communication with his parents remained crisp all well and prayer for good health for the family, one of his letter to his friend revealed his initial experience truthfully,

"The past few months have been traumatic: a period of loneliness, self doubt and constant unyielding pressure. The days seemed never ending. It was irritating to wait for sunset and roam round here and there to stay away from ragging even after the classes. On the study front, the topics of mathematics and physics were too fast as if passing over our head. And workshop, less said is better. For a great many of us there came moments often for the first time in life we would quite seriously wonder whether we would pass!"

Things however changed and per necessity the learning curve became steep. The result of the mid semester examination confirmed his aptitude and intelligence for higher studies and the result of the final examination was stunning. His friends, seniors and even a few professors who knew him congratulated for the grand result.

Every year the programme remained fully packed with activities: pressure of studies, activities like participation in annual function, model building, educational tour and industrial training. In addition, taking a dip in the Ganges, visit to Sarnath with friends kept him totally busy. When the time came for leaving after four years of intimacy, all were in coeval with the fact that the student life has already come to an end. And that they have to prepare for yet another phase of life. By His grace events turned in his favour: after the inexorable travail for four years amid social pressure and financial crunch he gained a professional degree from the most prestigious institute of the country with academic excellence- a rank in the university. He returned in the summer of 1967 educated, victorious, undaunted and thrilled to be home with a sense of accomplishment after long accomplished journey. He decided to a career as an engineer to be associated with nation building. He was overwhelmed by the writing of Pandit Jawaharlal Nehru, the prime minister of India, "Whenever I see these great engineering works, I feel excited and exhilarated. They are visible symbol of building up the new India and providing life and sustenance to our people."

PART THREE

Family and Profession

Act, act in the living present
Heart within and God's overhead
—Henry Longfellow

Wife, Sarala

A decisive moment in his life. He thought over and over. He has heard and overheard the continuing debate from people concerned and not-concerned about the future of his life: suitability of a less educated girl with a highly educated professional against offers aplenty. And he reflected, "The choice of mother and aunt, crafty and cautious women of their times in the given boundaries of their own penurious lives, they have never entertained abstract. They have observed her for years and found suitable in every way; plain, sober, pretty, penny-pinching and congenitally pessimistic. They could hardly appreciate compatibility." His friends described Sarala as a woman of stunning beauty, and one of them remarked, "My dear, I witnessed her the other day when she came with her friends to bathe and thirteen men fainted at the great pond from the sight of her maddening liveliness."

The circumstances compelled him to accept the proposition from the parents regarding the ceremony for consummating the marriage and he agreed to. He thought, 'he could now afford to be indulgent of that particular foible.' And even within the limits of domestic trivia where the rules set by Manu and Parasar still governed, their inevitable intimacy scented their dreams with all its powers. They entered a life endless, shadow less, boundless in duration as of an eternity and love in its sympathy, joy in its fullness. She was innocent, obedient and totally devoted. One morning she requested his mother to help getting absolution by taking *charanamrit* regularly after bath and offering to the Sun God and *Tulsi*. Days passed like hours and months like days. She, in the wings of an ancient, formidable instinct would rise up and drape her body over his, slipping him into herself with uncanny gentleness so as not to wake him completely and destroy the dream like sensation of the act, but to amplify it further into a deeper realm of mischief. Their forms, young and taught moved softly and silently. The body leapt to greet the counterpart, their scents mingled as the world seemed to pause to absorb their rhythm. The lips pressed, tongues met and the souls merged to unison. She closed her eyes, tighten herself around him and he gasped with his thumb at the base of her spine where it dimpled. It was the moment of ecstasy.

During the sojourn he understood her because like him she too was a victim of circumstance. He analysed her strength and weakness and concluded that closeness in spirit, thinking and perception was rather difficult. Incompatibility notwithstanding, he decided to accept her as the partner and try to mould her to the society she would have to interact. His friends and colleagues were flummoxed with the unique combination of her charm and his intelligent way of conducting. The life's journey continued. Their physical and emotional bond gradually strengthened, though perspectives remained distant.

As a natural process, it unveiled with gratifying clarity the siblings they have created: exquisitely molten eyes, fragile nose, moon face and clavicle of such elegance that lovers would expound their winged merits in later years from now. She mothered three daughters and a son. She was a proud mother of the cute kids who excelled in work and play. She too strived to satisfy their desire with love and affection.

Time passed. The siblings grew to attend university and live in hostels. And she was to be alone. While Bibhu had a job: office, friends she had only the home and children. Her educational background and limitation to learn different local languages posed problem. All those who were close were not alike. Some with similar background and bit of understanding became friends and their fractured English created a melody of its own and others who happened to be critical of her were disarmed before her childlike simplicity and delight. Everyone however appreciated her savoury dishes. She enjoyed cooking. To her it was an art, a kind of sorcery in the whole process: the choosing of ingredient, cutting or grating, as required, preparing spices, garnishing. Though some viewed as tiresome necessity, many felt the taste was due to her unconditional love in what she did. Those happened to have enjoyed asked for more and rest who only learnt expected to snatch the earliest opportunity.

Service Career

Bibhuti was ready to enter a new phase of life, different from the past with responsibility of a family thrust upon. Often wrapped in thought, he would issue from his solitary home early in the evening hour wondering along the narrow path to a wild and lonely spot that has struck his fancy in his rambling, seat himself on some fallen fragment of rock and burying his face in his hands, burrows puckered and remain for hours in quiet reflection, senses alive in anticipation thinking how to meet the expectation of the parents, relatives; friends and neighbours, sometimes oblivious that night has completely closed in and thick black darkness cast its spell on every object near by.

It was not opportune time, too. The economy of the country was in disarray due to wide spread draught consecutively for the past few years and the government remained occupied with arrangement of essential food items leaving the development programme to naught. Economists started describing the period as 'plan vacation'.

The avenue for employment for engineers remained limited to public sector steel plants and he has already appeared in the interview. He had long anxious moments: anxious for a job, anxious to decide how to take care of the diverse aspirations of the family and the inevitable problems of a family life comprising his simple, little educated wife in a foreign land with friends and colleagues whose spouses were by and large city bred, with modern styles, even though not well educated.

As a Teacher

The uncertainties, anxieties and apprehension came to an end. He received an offer of appointment as lecturer in the college he studied. He considered it God-sent: it would help him fulfill his personal dream for higher studies along with service essential to meet the family expectations. Declining other offers, he preferred to continue in the teaching profession. As he has already spent four years in the campus, it was 'home coming'. Life was as used to be, except that earlier he used to be busy with writing assignments and now time spent in correcting. His parents and wife were happy as he frequently visited home combining small holidays with leave and usual vacations of the academic institution.

The final examination was in process. A notice was served inviting all faculties that the director of the institute would meet the principals of college of engineering, college of mining and metallurgy and the college of technology over tea. It was clear that these colleges were integrated to one in the pattern of Indian Institute of Technology with a director as the administrative head, but no further details were available till everyone left home during the summer vacation. The next session commenced with a different note: many professors were not on the roles, the ad-hoc appointments were not renewed and a few regular appointments have been made during the vacation without any opportunity for those serving for the past three years. The new appointees were not rankers as those holding ad-hoc positions and the only reply available was that 'time has changed'. Sometime during the day, he sat on a marble bench of the university *Shiva* temple alone in a quietistic contemplation wondering at the strange world and thinking, "Wasn't it the same world where I had once discovered beauty, respected people and believed that service to fellowmen is service to God? Not even the life's blows had bestowed wisdom upon me- would I ever learn?"

Bibhuti was in great distress: no job, no application for job. And he mentioned to a senior professor with whom he was working, "I planned a long journey, but the train derailed even before it could pick up speed. Well, I don't know what is in store for me." The professors in the department were very sympathetic. In the circumstances, they advised all of them to get admitted in the post graduate programme as regular students. Some left for trying alternate avenues. He decided to continue with studies with the scholarship available for postgraduate students. Though routine attendance in class continued, he could not settle. The session ended. As usual he excelled in the examination. And perchance, he happened to meet the principal of one of the engineering colleges of his state. During a brief interaction he was impressed with Bibhuti and asked if he was interested to join as lecturer, which he readily accepted.

Consequent upon a thorough selection process, he joined as lecturer in the mechanical engineering department of the college. He had a lot of expectation to live with his own people in a friendly atmosphere. One of his friends was pursuing business in the city and helped him settle down. Within days the senior professors, the peers and students started liking him as a good teacher and a nice human being. The head of the department however nurtured a personal grudge, perhaps due to the fact that his consent was not taken for his appointment or attributable to his tunnel vision.

With the passage of time, his popularity in the college grew for his open minded attitude to help colleagues and students. He resolved to keep himself away from embarrassment, perform his duty quietly and unassumingly with hope that the ill feelings would die down in due course. The unexpected development took a different turn. Fighting back tears he narrated the incident;

"As I said, I accepted everything that came along without a complaint. Though the place seemed to be a weird combination of a sinister design and wicked plotting, a place full of terrifying intimidation of honesty, sincerity and academic excellence providing a numbing impact, perhaps with a purpose of embarrassing and ultimately throwing an 'outsider' or the nonconformist. But to me it was unwillingly fascinating. My objective was to spend a peaceful life. I think, it was winter time and the senior professors were on leave. The college used to conduct classes for AMIE students on various subjects. There was an honorarium of ten rupees per hour and the professors used to monopolize. And in their absence I was asked to take a few classes. The aspirants were relatively older, from the industry and pursuing the programme for promotion. My teaching was a good change for them, a departure from the usual monotonous note writing from the black board. They liked the way I explained, my approach and clarity. They petitioned to the principal that they preferred teacher like me for understanding the topic. The principal availed of the opportunity to tease the seniors and circulated the request. The incident sparked off yet another storm and by the time I learnt of the background it was too late. The authority began to rule; in many occasion I was asked to explain my action and life for me was almost strangulating. While I started preparing my strategy to meet the challenge, I received an offer to join Government of India as a class I officer on the basis of the result of the Engineering Services. I was a bit undecided as I abhorred routine and dreary paper work. The principal somehow learnt about this and advised me to accept the offer. It remains a mystery whether his advice was to get rid of the perpetual controversy or it was an honest decision. In any case, I wanted to live in peace and left the college."

As an Officer

From a quiet sleepy rural academic environment to an aspiring metro, with further ambition perhaps to make it big, he reached the national capital, Delhi on a mid summer night, alone. Help came from the most unexpected quarters. A co-passenger who was visiting Delhi for the first time offered to accommodate, though for a limited days. It was a respite. In his search for an abode he rediscovered Delhi – a city of 'dust and distance', though later Morarji Desai while giving up politics after a brief Premiership said, "I will never come back to Delhi again. It's a city of thieves and thugs."

The change from a quiet campus life to the metropolis in its extreme climate, full of indifferent people around was not so easy. His experience in the city, to begin with was too troubling: not a single soul he knew with whom he could share his feelings, traumatic search for a shelter in the exacting climate and above all the problem of food. Born and brought in rural background, education in small city, he learned to live a simple life that eluded him. All along he has been happy with movement in a bi-cycle and the exhausting travel to and fro office by city transport was a night mare. While he enjoyed a big official residence in a calm environment of the campus, he had to content with a small room without any independence.

He learnt and read that Delhi is a city of mysterious eternity whose old ruins proclaim a majestic and imperial past and the present pulsate vibrantly symbolizing not only the ever flowing life of India but also international culture. Situated on the bank of eternal *Yamuna* it has witnessed the glorious and tumultuous five thousand years of history that began with *Pandava's Indraprastha* and continued with the *Moghul* traditions and legacies of the British. Its myriad of faces was indeed fascinating: a city of gardens, of historical monuments, of people from different regions: turbaned Sikhs, *ghagra* clad *Rajasthanis*, glamorous *Kashmiris* and a cosmopolitan look with foreigners from almost every part of the planet. Its roads were often decorated with arches, flowers and national flags of India along with some other countries signaling the visit of their premier or president for bilateral and multilateral discussion. The demonstrations on the lawns around 'boat club' a sobriquet for a long artificial water mass with some boats for tourists and the utterances of the leaders generally heard from the office were interesting pastimes. It used to be occasion to see people of all shapes, sizes, ages, colours, backgrounds, interests, concerns and prejudices. In case one would have taken pains to chronicle these events even for a year it certainly would have been a best seller. The area now a days are prohibited by law for such gatherings except for the annual republic day parade and passing of VVIP cavalcades.

His office was situated in one of the central secretariat buildings on the Rajpath that provided a grotesque appearance to its visitors and awesome to onlookers. It has been a seat of power with half a dozen

PART TWO

Bibhuti's Education

If one does not know to which part one is going, no wind is favourable. —*Lucius Annaeus Seneca*

High School

The turn of event was a gift. A new high school started functioning a year back in a neighbouring district and a group visited the village in search for good students offering scholarship. Since finance was the impediment, the offer could not be opposed. It was a ray of hope in the horizon. In the midst of the desert of poverty and penury the opportunity was an oasis; a way to realising his dreams. He hoped, "Life's poetry would certainly bring into reality forcing forward step by step to the happiness which has once been lost." He visualized the road ahead and decided to walk along. He could not afford to stop. It was journey afresh.

It was Kumar High school. The school functioned in a six roomed building made of mud walls, tinned roof, of which four class rooms, one headmaster's office and another for the teachers. The furnishings in the class rooms limited to long benches and tables for students, one chair and a table for the teacher and black-board plastered on the wall. The background of the school was extensive *saal* (Shorea Robusta) forest. The location being away from the habitation provided a quiet environment, excellent for studies. There were eight rooms for the hostel, each accommodating ten-twelve boys. The hostel served only two meals, at 9 am/pm ministries their ministers and big bosses. The staffers however were no different. In any case, it was beyond Bibhuti's nature to look back and run away. He decided to adapt to the circumstances he was in and the journey has already begun.

During an introduction session, a senior officer asked, "Why did you come all the way to Benares for studying?" And he replied,

"I went to a reputed institute to acquire a credential- a degree in engineering that everyone believed would launch me into a stimulating and lucrative career."

"And how was the programme?"

He explained,

"Though the tough programme was not immediately compensated with expectation due mainly to the economic recession at national level for a long time, it certainly did equip us to face any challenge for leading pretty interesting lives. I am proud to be a graduate from such an institution. The faculty and associates are men of unusual intelligence and ability, constantly striving to adapt and improve an already remarkable system. I find myself looking back with a kind of awe at all that it taught me. Even today I see it with a golden haze of affection. I wish I could go back. But always apprehensive to the question, "How would you see yourself if you are asked to repeat the second year programme you entered?" And my response always would be to drop by knee and beg for mercy."

He learned later that he also passed from the same institute and wanted to learn the present scenario. And he was one of his well-wishers. A colleague who had joined a few months back explained his perception of the position that they were class I gazetted officers in the Government of India, one of the most exclusive enclosure of salaried elite and vested with authority hardly enjoyed by any other office. But he intoned, "What have I to do with powers?"

The sphere of official activities, as he was told was sublime: development of industry and technology in the country in coeval with the national policy perspective of 'self reliance'. Though the basic policy documents were 'The Industries (Development and Regulation) Act, 1951' and the annual 'Export and Import Policy' numerous amendments/clarification through notifications, circulars and instructions; some meant for internal use and some for the information of public flooded. A veil of secrecy regarding the rules and procedures prevailed partly due to the fact that hardly anyone could keep track of these changes and partly to take decision that others could not challenge. His learning experience however was exciting and bewildering: exciting because the new arena was far away from his academic background and baffling due to its language, too perplexing to conceptualize.

His initial experience continued to remain an enigma for sometime. The officers used to talk and gossip in informal groups, expressing feelings about each other: of obedience, pride, pain and indifference. But very little concern for the organisation they belonged. He perceived too soon that the office has been vested with enormous powers and manned with officials most of whom neither have the requisite academic background, experience nor the aptitude to solemnly accomplish the national task. They hardly cared to learn their role, relevance and overall perspective except taking decisions by virtue of authority conferred on the office. While the job demanded a unique combination of personal capacity, conviction and system compulsion, they seemed to be ever busy with 'file'.

The change from deriving solution on the principles of mathematics and application of science to taking decision with biased emphasis on 'precedence' and more so when the so called precedence was in accessible was too difficult to endure. The office too had no system of training the new entrants, leaving them to learn 'on the job'. A new officer had to content with the knowledge limited by his boss's, his attitude and his perspicacity about the young officer appointed directly to the status which he has attained through seer happenstance.

The time rolled on. Consequent upon the implementation of the recommendation of the parliament committee, officers from Engineering Services joined every year and the overall scenario of the office changed. They gradually made inroads to the affairs of the functioning of the organisation; formally as well as informally. Bibhuti took keen initiative and proved to be a capable in organizing in coordination with diverse views. He was accepted as the leader of the informal group to pioneer certain issues that confronted their organisation: a national level cadre service with organisation structure providing career prospects, proper working environment in office and maintaining hygiene.

In the mean time, he took admission to pursue the management programme on part time basis offered by the reputed institute in the capital. His wife and daughter also joined. His social circle expanded. Organizing the home in addition to the official and social responsibility kept him totally engaged. His journey in office was too tumultuous: very often he had to bear the torture of hostile bosses, work in extreme circumstances and above all his dreams for a career path shattered. He however continued with his own style of maintaining a supreme order. He loved having everything tidy, in its proper place and in control. He took pains to plan that helped him not to forget anything or miss anything important. He preferred a predictably efficient life. His memory was so prodigious that he has never forgotten anything. In any case, he got mired to the prevailing environment. By instinct, he was invariably friendly, courteous and considerate and on the whole he received high acclaim from the industry he was assigned to deal with and felt a sense of satisfaction.

On one occasion, he recounted a few incidents that affected his life:

"Well, seniority in any government department is very important because the whole environment is not conducive to reward the efficient and people in the higher management level prefer 'status quo'. By the time I realized, I may confess, it was too late. There were two other colleagues too. We joined this department based on our selection to the Railway Services and pushed here as the ministry wanted to fill up the vacancies soon. The administration however was unaware of the fact that merit alone decides the seniority in case of officers recruited on all India basis examination as against date of joining deciding inter se seniority as it used to be.

In compliance with the administrative and procedural requirement, we represented to the department for redressal of our grievance, but without any success. We were constrained to seek justice from the court of law. One of our colleagues approached a senior counsel of the highest court and he agreed to take up the case as he was convinced that ours was a 'cast iron case' and we were unnecessarily harassed. He decided that we petition the highest court against abridgement of fundamental right guaranteed under the constitution. We were excited to learn his independent view as he happened to be the chief justice of a high court. Naively we followed his advice. But as luck would have it, the senior of the two judge bench was an aspirant of the highest office and he couldn't take the risk of ire of the then emergency ruler that he has entertained a case against the government, despite its merit. Eventually he declined to admit the case. Well, the fact remained that our fate was decided by his attitude. It has been proved beyond doubt that attitude alone influences one's thought, feeling and action and person's behaviour pattern: cynical or trusting, experimental or conservative, concerned or malcontent could never prevent a person playing a role well if he has the right attitude. To quote Winston Churchill, "Attitude is a little thing, but makes a big difference."

The feeling of frustration led two other colleagues to leave for better opportunities elsewhere. I once again accepted the life as it is with determination to fight to finish in this unfriendly world."

He, in the mean time secured a post graduate degree in management. A promotion was also granted and he moved on in the bureaucratic ladder. One afternoon, sitting pensive he described how his effort to pursue research was made futile by the strange behaviour of people at the helm of affairs.

"There were many disturbing factors: Loosing the battle for restoration of seniority on merit, the bleak career prospect in the organisation due to indifferent approach of the administration regarding the cadre service and my strained relation with the head of the department. In this backdrop, I wanted to engage myself and satisfy with my yearning for higher studies. I applied for admission to the part-time Ph. D. programme of the most prestigious institute in the capital and succeeded. But the admission was subject to the condition of 'no objection' from my employer. I was very excited. I informed all: family, friends and well-wishers. We celebrated with our close friends of the 'tea club'. It was a happy moment. But as usual the joy of accomplishment was short lived. The administration denied to begin with. To their tunnel vision it was not necessary. In addition, the director of establishment was of the view that joining a higher study programme may hamper official duties. I could easily realize that beneath his dulled eyes lay a gleam which bespoke the not uncommon combination of self-importance and officious self-righteousness. But I was not sure, whether it was his idea or borrowed to satisfy his boss. I felt as if thousands of devils were conspiring against me. I confronted and with no plausible answer to my questions, a 'no objection' was finally granted with thirteen conditions which could not find favour with the director of the institute in spite of the pressing request of the head of the department. Well, I did to the extent it was possible and accepted the final decision as His wish. The exercise ended in futility."

Despite securing a coveted post graduate degree in management, it was not easy for Bibhuti to move out as nothing came across to his satisfaction. He continued to strive with all his sincerity. True to the dictum, 'when winter comes, spring can never be far behind' the luck seemed to favour a change he coveted. The chain of events that happened;

"On one early September morning the telephone rang. There was a discreet instruction,

"Please come to my room."

It was few minutes before ten and I could not even guess who called me. I was all alone in office. The atmosphere was quite serene except the sounds of occasional talk of the cleaning staff. I have been an early riser and ready for action when half of the world is in bed. I have developed this habit since childhood and still continuing. I therefore used to take an early chartered bus and reach office by quarter to ten when the office starts at quarter past ten. The half an hour used to be sufficient for me to organize for the day's work: prioritizing in the never ending flow to limit delay, delegating with instructions, if any and in-depth analysis, contemplation without disturbance for an optimal decision in certain tricky proposals.

"My boss used to be ready for work normally by eleven. May be he has some visitors and some urgent attention is required." I thought and proceeded to first floor, which is the seat of power in Udyog Bhawan accommodating more than fifteen ministers and a dozen secretaries. I peeped into his room and as usual it was empty. While I was about to come back, someone from the crossing called me aloud. I turned and he said, "Secretary is waiting for you."

I proceeded with him in supplication. Neither of us spoke as we were not so familiar. The secretary was new and so his personal secretary. As I entered his room and greeted, he offered me to take seat and said, "The executive director of the Indian Investment Centre is a friend of mine. He has requested me to send a good officer for his office. I think you are the kind of person he is looking for."

Before I could say anything, another senior officer entered with a few foreigners for their meeting with secretary at ten (pre scheduled) and by decorum, I had to exit, thanking him for the offer.

I thought I should first go to that office and learn what would be the nature of job prior to taking decision. But I was a bit worried, "Why he chose me? He does not even know me. We had interacted only once in a meeting." And keeping these to rest, I thought of visiting that office with a friend after tea. When I narrated the incident to colleagues with whom we take tea together at around eleven, a lot of hypothesis emerged, some in lighter vein and someone serious: 'You were too brusque in the meeting that day, he wants to get rid of you.' to 'He must have learnt from the previous secretary about your capability.'

The bizarre speculations came to rest when our peon came with an office order regarding my posting in the new office as Technical Advisor in a grade higher than the present. My boss took exception to the order that I have decided to leave the organisation without even informing him. I humbly explained the circumstance that I was asked to join an organisation about which I myself was not aware of. While he offered to stop the transfer, I thought of taking a decision only on evaluation of the pros and cons. As I realized I would gain about three hundred rupees a month and it would be of great help, I joined after a few days completing the work on hand.

A new chapter of my life began in so far the office and work was concerned though all other remained the same. I continue to travel in the same chartered bus a distance of two stops more without any additional fare."

He learnt that the office was incorporated as an association with the single objective to promote foreign investment in India including investment from the non resident Indians. The ministry of finance financed and eventually controlled its functioning. The head office was at New Delhi with five overseas offices and all officers were on deputation from other departments. The change from a powerful department to an office for promotion through information to prospective investors looked somewhat bizarre to many. He however accepted as a good change in spite of the fact that there was no scope for foreign posting at that stage. The job also involved publishing information literature on policy, procedure of the Government of India, organisation of seminars, workshops including conferences for visiting foreign delegations. His air of confidence with his brilliant academic background, conceptual clarity of policy/procedures and communicating promptly charmed all and the boss in particular. He equipped himself to serve the organisation on the premises that knowledge was his capital and information the business. And it paid dividends. Within weeks the whole office reposed confidence in him and he was called upon to handle any problem that required immediate attention. And time rolled on as usual. He and his family visited their native place during the summer vacation. By the time he was back in office, the executive director informed him of the good news of his posting at Frankfurt for which he has initiated action. He also asked him to keep the information to himself and prepare for joining as early as possible.

Tenure at Frankfurt

The decision of the office to post Bibhuti to the office at Frankfurt for three years on Foreign Service came as a surprise. In those days a foreign visit used to be a dream come true and posting without any lobby or contact was not heard of. In any event, it was exhilarating. His wife and children were too excited to learn that they would spend three years in Germany. Closing of their residence gleaned up over past thirteen years was not an easy job. Some of his friends helped to ease the situation. They agreed to keep some household paraphernalia for three years.

And on an early September afternoon, he along with his wife and three children arrived in Frankfurt with renewed enthusiasm to begin a new chapter. Selection of a proper accommodation for three years stay took a bit time. The normal routine commenced from the day one for Bibhuti. The girls were admitted to the international school even during their period of stay in hotel. The only problem to begin with was food; a change from the home cooked to European recipe. Taste apart, price too was prohibitive. Welcome dinners from some Indian officers were respite.

The reputation of the office was far from satisfactory, as he learned during introduction to related organisation. He could only assure the best services in days to come. Pursuing the noble rule, 'knowledge as capital and information the business' he set the stage afire for a vibrant office. His sincere effort paid dividends. The foreign as well as nonresident investors often sought advice. The relationship with relevant organisation, industry associations and chambers improved. Unexpectedly large numbers of promotional events were organized not only in Germany but also in other European countries like France, Netherlands, Switzerland, Belgium, Austria, Italy and Spain. Regular monthly offices started operating in a few locations including a permanent India Office in a southern state of Germany. On an occasion, after the official dinner, he candidly praised the Germans, "You Germans are makers and doers. You are born in business and development. Being practical is part of your culture. And once a German ventured to conquer the world. For Indians, it is just the reverse. Our history exalts the dreamers, the mystics and the poets. We traditionally tend to rationalize on the past heritage. The result is visible." And his popularity grew. He became a respected person in the industry and business circles. They relied on his advice.

While he got the opportunity to visit these countries on official tours, the family needed their share of quality time for a it of enjoyment and relaxation. It was a unique opportunity for the family to see a few places of importance in Europe like London, Rome, and Paris. Time and economy compelled for systematic planning of the visits: a trip to London passing through Holland during the tulip season and return via Belgium; visiting Rome and Vatican city en-route to home during a summer vacation; a sojourn to Munich, Saarbrucken and dark forest; a trip on the river main and picnicking in nearby gardens along with other Indian families were some major events. The children still remember the scenic beauty of tulip gardens against the skyline of windmills, the inside arrangements of the luxury tourist ship to London from Hook von Holland, the memorable sunset from the deck of the ship, scenic beauty of Salzburg, Austria, breathtaking loveliness of the reflection of ever green pines, dazzling white of the snow, lighter blue sky above combining with the calm sparkling blue of the lake in Switzerland and the like.

Satisfied with his overwhelming performance, the chairman and the executive requested him to continue for some more time; but he decided not to avail of the opportunity in the interest of the children education. He asked to be relieved as soon as their final examination was over so that they could be admitted in India.

Transfer to Kolkata

The decision of the office to post him at Calcutta (now, Kolkata) came after he was relieved from the Frankfurt office of the Ministry of Finance to revert back to the parent cadre. The arrangement for travel of the family including luggage have been for New Delhi. He and his family were happy to stay in the flat they have acquired and the children to return to the same schools from where they were transferred. Kolkata was an unknown destination except that it was nearer to his native place. Despite his request, the administration insisted that his services were essentially required for the new office in the north-eastern region to be operated from Kolkata and he had to join in the new office. A group of close friends who gathered in a party to welcome him and also bid farewell were skeptical, "It would be too difficult for you to adjust in Kolkata after a long stay in Europe."

And his calm reply was, "The order of the cruel commander to a vanquished fighter to march to the frontier. What choice do I have?" And segued the discussion quoting an Arabian saying, "Mortals, if thou wouldst be happy, change the home frequently; for sweetness of life is variety and novelty. The morrow is not mine or thine." Finally masking his emotions, he intoned, "I always follow the dictum 'Onward, onward! Don't look back."

After week long toil at Delhi in the sultry month of July making arrangements for custom clearance of his belongings, transportation to new destination and travel arrangements, the family arrived in the 'City of Joy' in one rainy afternoon. He once expressed his first impression of the easten metropolis;

"The reception was more than I ever expected. The colleagues of the new office, the land lord family and a few friends helped me to settle down. There were however a bit of problem with regard to the admission of the children and I had to approach a number of schools in different part of the city. The life gradually settled to routine. My first impression of the city:

To my eyes Kolkata, Job Charnok's city was beautiful, even wild and exciting: the buildings of the British Raj stood side to side with modern mirrored business towers and haphazard slouch of neglected tenements. Shops, restaurants, hotels and kiosks filled the streets; every shop featuring smaller sub-shops attached to the front and generally encroaching the narrow footpath. The lanes and by-lanes too were crowded with vendors. The most bewildering sight was that people on the roads were cooking, eating and even rearing kids. High pitch music, aroma of spices, dizzyingly delicious fragrances and vibrant colours filled the environment. The only open space, *Maidan* too occupied with vendors, beggars, jugglers, acrobats, magicians, snake-charmers, messagers, astrologers, palmists, pimps and pushers and above all the vagrants sleeping on the verdant grass under the tree oblivious of the time and space. But all in harmony and mostly smiling."

He attended office with regularity and punctuality. His strict discipline, sincerity to the assignment, official rectitude and above all humane aspect of his personality were appreciated by peers, superiors, staff and the industry. Incessant rain during the monsoon period, busy streets, problem of commutation particularly for the children to school bothered him. Fortunately, he could get an official accommodation in the central part of the city that eased the situation. The routine work continued. The bleak promotion prospect in the organisation remained a cause of concern and anxiety. The wait ended. And one fine afternoon, he received a call from the Ministry Of Commerce that the selection process was complete with the approval of the competent authority and he should join their Export Processing Zone Office immediately. He recollected his application long back which has since been forgotten. The office happened to be in the same premises where he lived. He along with a colleague decided to visit the office same afternoon, incognito to access the situation and it was indeed revealing. The languid office environment, officials chatting in groups over tea when they should have been busy were discouraging. Well, he accepted the offer again for a change from the routine and as a challenge.

True to his nature he joined the office like a gust of fresh air and surprised all; the ministry, the industry, other offices with whom they frequently interacted with and the staff with his brisk business like style of functioning, almost on-line decision making, procedural streamlining and compassion. He listened to all and solicited everyone's co-operation for a new beginning. His dedication, clarity of objective and action had overwhelming demonstrative effect on the staff. Within a short span, the efficient management, exceptional response from the office in the slow paced environment became talk of the business circle to the pleasant surprise of all concerned. Words of mouth spread and proposals and entrepreneurs started pouring in, some with genuine projects and a few to validate what they have learnt. Intent notwithstanding, all received that same attention, required information and transparent decision. The assignment was full of authority, responsibility that involved innovative practices. With the exception of one, the whole office was inspired to act in the overall interest of development. The performance had the critics in despair and the admirers in raptures. And it continued for almost six years. In the process of his tumultuous journey, he could safely conclude that the enigmatic politicians and men in administration were persons whose grandeur was due to pomp of power and not of the light of thought. They unlike normal human characters lacked sensitiveness to others feelings: idiosyncrasies of affectation or obedience, pride or pain and never even cared to disguise hypocrisy and perfidy. Amidst all pleasures even a bit of pain stings. So was the situation: he described the behaviour of one of his staff members that he was sore with;

"It pains me to narrate an incident that involves one of our staff whom I helped out of the way to transfer to our office and post him such that he was at ease, living with family to take care of his handicap child and old parents. A bit of flexibility was also allowed so that he could resolve the problem he faced. I found him happy as time passed. After about a year, during my visit to ministry a senior officer called me and shown me an unsigned complaint, specifically against me. As he knew me well, he laughed at the letter and placed in the waste paper basket. He however cautioned me to be careful with the miscreants, too. I felt hurt, for it was totally false allegation. I investigated and surprised to learn with sufficient evidence that the letter was typed from our office and it was the work of two and one of them was the staff in question.

I wondered, "Why a person who has been benefited by me indulges in such activity?" Well, I had no answer. Conflicting emotions: action or let go, however burdened my mind for some time. Finally I opted for 'let go' thinking that the behaviour of a person is influenced by his own gloom and he covertly acts for some sadist pleasure, not joy of life."

Bibhuti's ardent faith in *karma* however could not deter him from proactive action even without any recognition. One of his colleagues once described how he won the hearts of all on the day of farewell.

As to his nature he said crisply, "I would quote Tagore whom we hold in reverence to present symbolically my work and my expectation: "I wanted to offer thee a flower, but I felt my whole garden be thine." and "My offerings are too timid in comparison. Therefore, you may remember them." And it remained deep in their memory.

Apart from office, his social life too was extremely engaging. When he joined the ministry, it was considered one very stabilizing factor that he would stay fixed in Delhi so long he has not decided otherwise. Now that he is in the city nearest to the hometown, his parents were excited: he would meet them more often, particularly on festivities which he has missed so far. He too thought of inviting near and dear ones on peregrination and satisfying some of their desires of travelling, visiting, shopping and getting a feel of life and activities in a metropolis, which they have heard a lot about, but had no opportunity to experience. And many a visits as well as invitation materialized in due course.

He too had to take care of the interest of his family members. He planned short tours to the shrines like Baidyanath Dham, Shakti Pitha, Puri, Konark, Iscon Temple at mayapuri and Nadia in addition to tourist attraction such as Darjeeling, Guruji's Shantiniketan and tea gardens of Bengal. The marriages of the daughters were also solemnized. Proximity to home helped him taken care of certain initial problems that normally arose when an educated girl with a back ground of total freedom joins an orthodox family enveloped in restrictions meant only for the new daughter-in-law.

Needless to say, the eighties were very different. The nineties witnessed a lot of changes for him in office as well as home front: an official foreign visit on invitation, assuming charge in a new office, daughters' marriage, preparing children entering professional institute for higher studies, sad demise of revered father. Every incident has been laden with sweet – sour memories; emotional to adventurous and tragic to nostalgic.

In Delhi Again

The extended period of his tenure came to an end and he reverted back to his parent department.

The department no doubt remained the same but the august office he joined was no longer in existence. Though some of his friends were happy with the changed scenario, he remarked, "Well, we have lost our identity and it is a great loss. A sense of identity makes an important contribution to the strength and warmth of our relationship, enrich our bond. As I see, we are not the same as used to be. The enthusiasm, vibrancy, spirit and excitement for action are nonexistent." In due course they too acquiesced the effect of change.

Sad Demise

His return and getting settled was smooth, a home coming. The major problems of Delhi have been taken care of; he had a flat of his own and no school going children. But anxieties would never leave him; his loving mother debilitated. Thanks to the rural telecommunication system that he could remain in contact. And suddenly one day she too passed away. He along with his family reached immediately for the last rites. His heart sank to visualize a parentless home. And he lamented, "Oh mother, would I ever have thy charm that touched my heart like the first ray of the sun? My life started with those golden gifts: your eyes;

calm, serene and deep, your soothing voice and above all your healing touch!" While returning, he told a friend, "Everything remaining same, I wonder why my perception gives a different impression?"

And at Delhi, wife started feeling weak with the menopausal syndrome setting in. In spite of treatment from the best doctors in town her health deteriorated. Amidst all this she exuded an extraordinary charm, with a smile that she wielded all her life and even now in her fifties, age and sickness had not failed her. The disease however moved inexorably along her nerves like a predator, spreading at its own pace not hers. It appeared from the casual approach to her failing health that she had made up her mind and wanted to die even without a fight. The date with destiny arrived and when the doctor broke the news to him, he stood transfixed tears rolling ceaselessly. One of his friend and his daughter present could not imagine that a man tough and strong at the surface could be so soft at the core. A large number of his friends came to offer condolences and he bravely philosophized quoting a poem of A.C. Maffen,

"Our life is but a winter's day:
Some only breakfast and away
Others to dinner stay and full fed;
The oldest man but sups and goes to bed:
He that goes soonest has the least to pay."

Some of his friend remembered to have heard him intoned, "*Our world will never be same again.*" She only left behind her saga to be remembered.

Life has always been a struggle for him, but this was a unique challenge. He once described,

"I continued living with the secret happiness of sweet excitement in the memory of her presence, soft touch, warmth of embrace. As I closed the eyes, her glowing face, petal lips would appear in a redolent pool bestowing tenderness in my heart and I could feel that the entire cosmos belonged only to me. There used to be moments particularly in the darkness of the night, I had to listen to the silence. I drifted from one place to another always seeking, searching and never finding. When I returned, there was no one to ask 'how are you'. No one to share a mood of pleasurable relaxation. No one cared a damn. I would have scarier yet, but goodness prevailed: I learnt to accept life as it is and readied to face with a new perspective and action. We perhaps met to create memories and parted to preserve them." And he said matter of factly, "in any case, I have to conduct myself being alone but not lonely".

PART FOUR

Living by Choice

They are never alone that are accompanied with noble thoughts. —*Sir Phillip Sidney*

Retirement

A time comes in everyone's life when he has to leave. And in government service it is by statute. A form is filled on the day of joining where the date of superannuation is to be stated. In his case there has been a bonus of two years, he has stated many a times. On the pre ordained day, even in the dim environment of the truncated office that engulfed the technical officers all were excited to meet and bid farewell to one of their beloved friend and colleague. Emotional words were spoken and as a mark of respect for his erudition, a statue of *Saraswati* was presented. One of his colleagues recounted his experience, "Almost all of us wondered to know the secret of his so simplistic as well as steadfast behaviour that hardly deviates from principle: whether he borrowed the terrible honestness from Gandhiji or the values has been imbibed in his character. And I am glad to say his actions have always been admirable."

A few of his friends came to his residence and he spoke to them in his literary style over a cup of coffee, "Tomorrow, the sun will rise to see a new phase of my life".

Following the man of wisdom that 'we should take pleasure to do what makes us happy' he devoted himself to reading and writing which he was very fond of and from these tastes arisen his principal enjoyment. He however opted to continue with his normal routine: habit of 'early rising', morning exercise, household chores, evening walk and pursuing hobby. Time got adjusted to the new schema and his confidence dictated to be prepared to walk alone, as always.

On a lazy leisurely afternoon one of his friends dropped by and to his surprise he was called upon to answer, "Have you ever thought of the people you have loved and lost long ago, particularly when you are alone?' And finding him apoplectic to such a queer pitch, Bibhu spoke, "It is quite possible that the comfort you draw from the memories would definitely be better to have loved and lost than to have never loved at all." He paused and added, "Recollection, though sometimes painful would continue to intrude which cannot and ought not be repelled."

Diverting from the philosophical, both friends then chitchatted over tea on matters of common interest. While explaining his occupation in the days after retirement he reflected, "My wife is no more to complain about my inattentiveness and the children are sufficiently grown up to appreciate." And his friend could instantly feel the silent sufferings latent in those words.

He again intoned,

"Our human condition makes us tend to share only the best of ourselves, because we are always searching for love and approval. But it is the law of nature that sometime we win and sometime we lose. Life becomes easy when we shift a bit of our perception: not to expect to get anything back, not to expect recognition for the effort, not that the genius would be discovered or would be understood. There is need to complete the circle, not out of pride, inability or arrogance, but simply because the existing things no longer fit in one's life. Pragmatism demands; clean the house, get rid of the dust, choose the door, change the record and stop being who you were, become who you are."

He then remembered Radhakrishnan's life inspiring thought, "Life is like a game of bridge..we did not invent the game or design the cards. We did not frame the rules and we cannot control the dealing. To that extent, determinism rules. But we can play the games well or play it badly. A skillful player may have bad hand and yet win the game. A bad player may have a good hand and make a mess of it. By exercising our choice properly, we can control steadily all the elements and perhaps eliminate altogether the determinism of nature."

And finally concluded,

'A tiny change of perception would make all the difference: to assign meaning and importance to each moment. It means being fully present in each moment because only the present moment truly exists. It means stopping to notice the beauty and love around us, within us: Many of us worry about future, hold inquest of the past and completely ignore the living present."

Though the delicacy and complexity of the intimate conversation between friends continued with interplay of gravity and playfulness, it conveyed an intense feeling of determination that he has acquired over the time.

As usual the discussion turned to the children and both exchanged a note of deep satisfaction over their performance looking forward to their bright career path. He accompanied his friend for some distance, bade him good bye and walked towards the neighbourhood park. Instead of the usual stroll, he sat down on an unoccupied bench, looked around and meditatively thought over the retirees around. His mind transgressed to his usual observation and he conjectured.

"Of the many retirees from different walks of life: service retirees, smart, clipped and distinguished, government retirees, smart, unclipped and distinguished and company retirees, smart; all mingle and coalesce among themselves with much banter and jollity, for all of them have one thing common: they possess rich experience of life and profession in their respective fields and eagerly await for people to ask for free advice – a novel way to spend some quality time. They however tend to forget that generation next is smart and as Abraham Lincon implied, 'people are smart most of the time and manage to escape the offers of free advice'. In stead they try to advise on food, exercise, sleep, medicine which the old folk take pride in comparing along with the anecdotes on how they outsmarted 'boss' in their journey. All such moments are in any case occasional and take limited time from the long stretch of the day. The activities are far and wide: some garden, some dose, some read, a few try to write; some play card, some do not play and some cannot play; some wonder what to do and more keep on wondering; some join NGOs and still some spend time watching TV.

In any event one has to live and why not live fully? I am reminded of Emily Dickenson, "To live is so startling, it leaves little time for anything else." And to live there has to be a purpose and fortunately I have one."

With this solemn determination he continues his journey further: to live a lie by choice. He once expressed his satisfaction for the opportunity to pursue the creative urge, "About my writing, I have written a lot before usually with a flair and ease; as a student, as a teacher, as an official all for a definite purpose. The writing now is perhaps to satisfy an urge to express and share thoughts with some one in the midst of a life of quietistic contemplation that I now devote myself. Though a poor substitute for a human ear, it is perhaps the only alternative. And in the December of my life the sense of limited time urges me on..."

And one of his teachers described him, "He stands alone as an oak amongst my students with his energy, capability, courage, willingness to learn and his indomitable determination, passion, compassion and strength of character that inspires all." It truly captures his personality.

Introspection

The author was too happy. His goal seems achieved. He has completed the manuscript. A larger audience would have the opportunity to visit the life and activity of a person who lives the way he likes. He is the hero whom he adored. He proceeded to surprise with the information. Sun was about to melt down in the western sky. Despite the silhouetted metro horizon, the changing hues were visible. He was reminded of the approaching dusk when he along with friends used to return home from school and face stiff opposition from the stead fast marching of the cow herd spreading dust, unconcerned with others convenience. And how they used to hurry to reach home and succumbed to innocent calves. How idyllic the experience indeed.

He thought of describing his friend of his nostalgia and walked to find him smiling with the flowers, singing in the soft breeze or seated fully emerged amidst the sweet fragrance of the *champa* and *chameli* in thegarden he nurtured with tender care. But to his surprise, the atmosphere was sombre. He realized that lone man's desperate attempt for passion and happiness brought bubbling to the surface the shameless whose insensitiveness has shattered his peace. The kinder circles would have asked 'what kind of compassion the society, the near and dear ones are capable of in return to his sacrifice and support?'

As always, he continued to be philosophical. He intoned, "There seems to be a mysterious pattern of return in human life. To some much is given. Of others much is expected. And as far as I am concerned, I do have a rendezvous with destiny."

He continued, "Memory fresh and overflowing with lifetimes experience: visual, auditory, chemoreceptive, tactile and kinesthetic- all frightened with nuances of emotion, heart filled with poetic thoughts, mind calculation and emotion, intuition tells me something I overlooked, something I forgot and directs me to follow, explore and find out. And I tend to attach meaning to every word and bits of sensory information in search of logical interpretation even from remote connections to gain insight."

The author was stunned to listen, "Will anyone mourn at my death?"

He conjectured the introspection has perhaps been doe to some developments which he is not aware of and it must have been a blow to his belief. But he preferred not to delve into, for the present and thought of calming him and tried to put in perspective that 'almost all who are acquainted with him like him and that he continues to be a source of inspiration for the young generation'. But before he could express, he had to listen to his analysis;

"Well, wife perhaps would have shed a few tears as I have been remembering her. But alas, she is no more.

Children; they hardly have time. They seem immersed in their dutiful life as they have been imbibed with the values; sincerity, honesty and 'work is worship'. I feel accomplished seeing them happy. I pray for their success and prosperity.

Brother and sister; they remembered me when they needed me. Today, with His grace, they are happy, busy with family and activities. I wish them good luck.

Relatives are many, some near and some afar. They would certainly demand a nice feast and new clothes for them and their family from my children. It's the wont after all.

And friends; by the time they learn about, it would be too late for even expressing a formal condolence.

Last but not the least, is the garden that I have nurtured as my children. They are with me all along, in sun and rain. Here too the trees have grown up and become self supporting. I have enjoyed the shade, the fragrance of the flowers and the fruit. It's too much to expect any more. The plants however need my care to grow and blossom. I have shared with them my lonely moments. They may cry for water on a sunny afternoon and feel the gardener missing."

The author thought to himself, 'there are moments in life that comes which cannot be prevented.' and ventured to sum up,

"I think, you have followed the path once traversed by a Greek youth, Icarus to reach for the sun oblivious of the fact that the wings are fashioned by wax. The contrast however is that he was at least warned by his father, Daedalus and you have been all alone vaulting with ambition to bring smile on as many faces. I consider your spirit honourable and failure, if any, would be memorable."

Things never stood still, not even in paradis.

—Albert Einstein

22

Living with Loving Memories

Love is composed of a single soul inhabiting two bodies.

—Aristotle

Nature is its own master. It obeys its own laws perfectly: the night falls, spreads its wings asking the mortals for a good night's rest, perhaps letting them to prepare for an active day while the stars play to the susurration of the wind; the stars fade, eastern sky changes its hues heralding sunrise that gradually washes the violet and pink to blue and it continues.

Man is ever dependent: his body sustainable by nature and perishable at His will; mind filled with extraneous perceptions; soul a part of the eternal *parambrahma* and a critical balance of the body-mind-soul keeps it going.

Srikant, one among myriads of His creation, has journeyed through the innocent childhood (*Satya Yug* of life), dreamy adolescence (*Treta*) and now in the period of activity (*Dwapar*), though youthful vigour is on the decline. He has been maintaining the balance to date, pursuing active habits he acquired since child hood: to wake up at the wee hours of the morn, enjoy nature's serene beauty and tranquility, listen to bird song, admire the vastness of the sky and above all, live a life of purpose. He valued principles, followed the happiness *mantra*:

Live simply,

Give more and expect less,

Free mind from worries, and

Fill the heart with love and compassion.

Life seemed so ornate: a happy family with an ever caring wife and mother, children to be proud of and near ones in harmony. He has, to a large extent also made conscious effort to correct the course based on the learning experience for a blissful life.

The wheel of life can never ever be up; and a day arrived when the indelible tragedy struck like a bolt from the blue. The lovely span of married felicity abruptly came to an end without any notice. They (Srikant along with his wife Swapna and daughter) had dinner together the previous night and retired. She slept with no complaints. The following fateful morning, she did not wake up. When called, she blinked. She was rushed to the emergency of the All India Medical Institute. A senior colleague and their daughter accompanied, only to wait outside. While there was hardly any information from the pachyderm medicos except 'please wait', Srikant prayed for her recovery tears rolling down.

Time is heartless and motionless when one wants it to move and save the one for whom one waits. The tensions of the minutes kept ticking; it seemed eternity. The final verdict came. 'And the walls came tumbling down...' His personal world shattered. The days of togetherness came to an end. Sorrow swept him off. All the philosophy failed the moment the dear one passed away. The Lord did not listen. It was preordained. Yes, 'the moving finger writes, and having writ moves on, not all thy piety nor wit shall lure it back to cancel half a line nor all thy tears wash out a word of it'.

They returned back. They had to. But she did not return with them. It seemed imposed on him that the rest of life be the reminiscence of their togetherness. He expressed his threnody to one of his colleagues, "Life seems empty. Death robbed me of her human presence and since then she seems so near and yet so far, so real and yet so remote for living rest of my life with her loving memory. But I pray her soul rest in peace."

The day next, a close colleague saw him in dolour, sleep-starved, enveloped in gloom and to divert his attention, took him to the park in front. They discussed the plans for funereal service, arrival of his son and other schedules. And to provide a bit of strength at such low time, he said, "I have seen you so strong capable of carrying through hurricanes. You have the children to take care of. Everything will be alright. It is His wish and we have to honour."

"I tell our love and life together and you would appreciate." he intoned and elaborated,

"Ours is a unique love story. It developed spontaneously and consummated with everyone's blessings. I fail to understand, why should it end so abruptly?"

He paused and continued, "I would begin with the

beginning. I was in Tenth class and she entered high school, class Eight. She was the daughter of the best teacher of the school. It so happened that the teacher developed a liking for me as a good student and asked me to join the group of students in his tuition class and get doubts clarified. His intentions were noble: to assist me honing my skills in understanding and writing and secure better position in the final Board examination. In our time, the high school was up to class eleven and there was two more years.

A few days passed. But I did not turn up. One day at the end of the school, he enquired again. I maintained silence. He understood and asked me to request my father to meet him when he visits next. When my father met, he requested him to permit me to join. He explained that it was in my interest. My father expressed his inability to pay for tuition as the hostel expenditure was burdensome. He laughed and said, 'He is such a brilliant student. I don't want any fees. It's free.' My father again politely declined. And it was finally settled that I would take care of the studies of his children for an hour and join his class for an hour, in return.

The headmaster had a different point view: a good student should not waste time amidst family disturbance; he ought to concentrate on studies and doubts could be cleared in class. But hesitantly permitted me to join his class in the morning. Every morning, I would reach early and assist his daughter in class Eight and son in class Five. During the course of the routine, we, myself and Swapna were attracted to each other. It was too natural. In the guise of some assignment to be completed, she would request me to come after the class and we continued our chit-chat. On festive occasion, her mother would ask me to come in the evening for pooja and Prasad and I welcomed to be near her as long as I could.

The summer vacation was important to me and I was supposed to revise the course and proceed ahead with syllabus. But it was too difficult. I lost my usual concentration and remained preoccupied with the outcome of our feelings. I thought, 'if I don't put an end to such state of my mind, I would be doomed. I was afraid of being pilloried as a poor peasant's son and aspiring for the moon. We may have our feelings, but social norms certainly dictate otherwise.'

After the vacation, not to the joy of either, I behaved different: relation strict to studies. I reduced my visit to twice a week and after some time, to once a week pleading for burden of preparation for the final. The year passed. I could not resist meeting her. We searched for opportunity to be together and our intimacy grew. I vividly remember the evening before I was scheduled to leave the hostel for good. I went to pay my obeisance to my revered teacher, his wife and bid good bye to the children, my students. But I could not find Swapna. I waited a bit and left.

It was end February, official spring season. The night was mildly cool and pleasant; the atmosphere wildly scented. The moon, a discernible slice was silently playing hide and seek with the floating clouds. And to my surprise, she was standing under the canopy of the leaves in dappled moon light on the side of the lane. My heart started beating fast. My fervent desire for the soft touch, warm breath and dissolve in the union to eternity grew intense. The principles, I valued prevented me from such misdemeanour.

"I was searching you to say good bye." I said.

She looked at me, askance. A feeling of profound disquiet of unexpressed emotion pervaded. Eyes spoke. Both fought tears. The stars watched and waited to listen. Neither I could say a word, nor she dared. I was a victim of perceived normativism and she was trapped in social conservatism.

Deep inside, I felt a wave of melancholy and left gazing up at the stars. While leaving, she put a handkerchief on my hand and intoned, "Please do remember and visit us. All of us like you." It was scented with her usual perfume and she painstakingly inscribed 'S&S' on one corner. I still possess it as a souvenir of our true love.

And our feelings got buried in the secret chambers of our hearts.

The night, after the farewell dinner, all final year students could not sleep and assembled in one room. A few of our close friends also joined. We talked, laughed, cried, hugged and promised to meet again. And during the course of pranks and teasing, one of my classmates who happened to be too jealous of me made a slanting remark, 'You would certainly come back here, Pussy Cat, to meet the queen.'

And I replied, "My future is uncertain. You all know my financial status. I may have to search a teacher's job in a village primary school and settle with the ordinary. Queen and me are a horizon."

Revelation of the stark reality touched everyone's heart. Almost all had to fight tears and drift to humour.

The next morning we parted laden with memories exclusive to each one.

Fortunately, by His grace I began my journey to the university education. Those of my classmates, who had finance, could not secure admission and the majority in penury had to settle with any job at the earliest opportunity. Amidst intense activity, the school life that comprised our adventure, drama, picnic including personal indulgences relegated to oblivion.

Our feelings did fade to a great extent due to remoteness but remained alive in the corner of heart to surface at the times of aloneness. As a student in the University for long years, I had had occasions to meet a number of girls. Some expressed desire to be close, but the first love in life overwhelmed. I could not think of developing another relation. Yes, 'first' in everything has a special place in life; like the first day in school, the first salary cheque, first story in print and the like. And the first love, perhaps infatuation, or might have been ethereal, enjoyed a unique position.

Six years passed. I completed my engineering. When I returned home, mother informed that father has settled a bride for me. "It's too soon, maa. Let me get a job, start living and be capable of taking the burden of a family." I pleaded.

"We have full faith in your capability. She is a good girl and you know her." mother quipped.

Though I wanted to learn more about, modesty prevented me to ask. The same evening father explained me that a proposal has come from my teacher for the marriage of their daughter with me. He asked, "If you have no objection, I will consent. I was waiting for you to arrive." The information levitated me to seventh heaven. Though from a practical point, I wanted time to discuss with her and evaluate her compatibility in our environs, neither my parents nor hers thought it was necessary.

The marriage was solemnized and consummated. I was scared; she would find it difficult to adjust and there would be tension. But nothing of sorts happened. She became the loving one for all: our family, relatives, neighbours and friends. She charmed with her behaviour, action and intoxicating smile. Her strength and adroitness to adjust astonished me. We promised to be together to the end in pleasure and pain, in hope and despair. We lived together for 33 years in blissful wedlock.

Dear, this was our life that ended."

"I wish I could share your suffering. The situation demands that you have to put a brave front in the spirit of what you always value, 'what cannot be cured has to be endured'. You have responsibilities; you are now both mother and father to the kids." He advocated.

"Yes, time would pass and I'll tend to reconcile with the eternal truth: where there is life, there will be death. The boundaries of her presence and absence will also blur, but the memories of our sharing and caring will be an elixir. I have faith in the Divine and I am sure, I'll hear the laughter echoing through the firmament when I need company." Srikant stated and became pensive, but thought it prudent to maintain optimism and accept reconciliation in an indeterminate future.

The funereal, rituals were completed with the help of the friends and colleagues. He joined duty. He was determined to move forward. Nobody could notice any change in him but himself. A state of privation invaded him; he could not even shed tears before the children and had to search for solitude.

By the time he was mired to the new life, the official activity came to an end. He retired. Those who knew him were confident that 'the strength of his character has been tested time and again. He has by and large come out successfully not only in good times, but being resilient through the periods of crisis. He is seen committed to core Gandhian principles and values'.

He stepped into a new phase of life: the debilitating old age (*Kali Yug*). In his characteristic style, he turned the challenge to opportunity; utilizing the independent status to pursue a passion he yearned but never had time. Despite available alternate facilities, he preferred to live alone, for he desired his own space. A new chapter began. Another routine followed. His experience, fresh and anew has been inspiring and he learned a new dimension of enjoyment.

A day in his solitary life; wake up early, by habit; go for the morning-walk, join the group to spend some time; interact with children, friends, relatives, thanks to the telephone to keep connected; occasionally meet colleagues formally as well as informally in addition to his normal chores and neotic pursuit. And in lone moments, he drew solace from the reminiscence of the past that mirrored off and on in forms and nuances - break from the monotone.

Time spares none: winter has to give in to spring and spring to summer; a child becomes adult and gradually grows old which even the advance science has not been able to counter yet. Srikant is no exception